MW00743615

Copyright © 2010 Charly Rasheed

Brain Alignment: The Art of Focus in Tennis

ISBN 1452833079

dedication

I would like to dedicate this book to my parents, Emile and Donna Rasheed, for nurturing my love for the game of tennis and to my two sons, Ian and Isaac, for helping me to further conceptualize the game of tennis, thereby enabling me to pass my comprehension on to them.

TALENT
Shawn Harris, Shaw Tharpe, Martin Zumpft

PHOTOGRAPHER
Jodi Niswonger

GRAPHIC DESIGN
Nikki Villagomez

REFERENCES
Kristi Holliday, Kristie Santora

REFERENCES
Dr. John Baird, F.A.A.F.P., Dr. Francis X. Walton, Psychologist

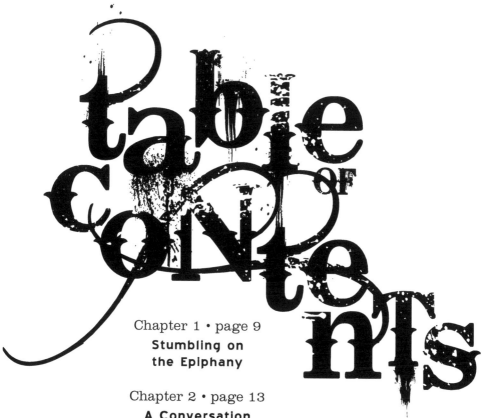

table of contents

Chapter ne

Stumbling on the Epiphany

Roger Federer's influence on the game of tennis stretches further than the historical implications. His technical approach to tennis is virtually flawless. Most notably, Federer's visual control at contact point is profound and something which, as a competitor and instructor, I became very interested. At some point, no matter what ball sport we have ever participated in, we have been on the instructional receiving end of "Keep your eye on the ball." Not until recently have I realized the significance of this instructional point, thus, opening up a system of thought, a psychology of sport, that shows us why this game of tennis is so mental.

Charleston, South Carolina is one of the state's and southern section's hot beds for tennis. The weather, the coast, and the abundance of phenomenal facilities combine to produce an environment of a tennis Mecca. In conjunction with these fantastic regional amenities are a small army of tennis directors and instructors. For the better part of a decade, The Charleston Professional Tennis League (CPTL) has provided a venue for these ex-collegiate and ex-professional tennis players to compete in the fall months of each year in a team format. In 2008 we included a singles element in the format of our CPTL season for the first time. I like doubles, however, I love singles. As one of five team captains, I had the responsibility of drafting my team. The draft is set up in a "waterfall" style so whether you have the opportunity of picking first or last your team should be equally fortified. Because I knew I wanted to play the number one singles position on my team, I recruited guys I knew were strong in doubles. This way I could maintain my singles position throughout the course of the season without conflict. In my first singles match of the season, I tripped over a technical fundamental of tennis and landed in a pool of questions whose answers opened a realm of thought that have since expanded my mental horizons.

Peak season at Wild Dunes Resort, located in Isle of Palms, South Carolina, is traditionally Memorial Day weekend through Labor Day weekend. As Director of Tennis at Wild Dunes Resort, I couldn't be in a better spot. Hundreds of new faces and new energies grace our eighteen court facility each week for three months straight. In our peak season of 2008, I was on an instructional kick of "eyes on contact." It was a great tip considering my market; people I would only see for a week. I always try to implement instruction that would not compromise what they would hear at home from their local pro. My biggest pet peeve, as an instructor in non resort settings, was my students going on vacation to resort settings and instructors filling their heads with information that would contradict or inhibit their current learning curve. Because I was ultra sensitive to this issue, when I became the Director of Tennis at Wild Dunes, it was my mission to find instructional points that could only compliment the instructors back home.

As I would feed my first round of balls to my clinic group, I would express the importance of "eyes on contact" and let everyone know how interested I was in that moment. Without fail, student after student, clinic after clinic, day after day, week after week, month after month I realized no one, even after I would tell them to have their "eyes on contact," could execute this most important fundamental of the game. This fact only strengthened my approach to this instructional point. At best, after a week of my instruction, I could make my students aware that they were not watching contact, but I did not have the ability to teach them to have "eyes on contact" every shot they would hit. I am very passionate about playing the game of tennis, but my true passion is instruction. The connection I have with the student is intimate, personal, and unique when they feel success through instruction. I started to realize "eyes on contact" was making my students aware of failure versus experiencing success. This was not acceptable in my world of teaching.

Our CPTL season in 2008 began shortly after our peak season concluded. I was going into my first singles match against a player that had recently graduated from the University of South Carolina as an All-American singles player. I am ten years his senior and on paper I didn't have a shot at winning. I am always interested in learning and exploring the competitive process which is why I would put myself in such a predicament. My mission in the match was to focus on contact just as I instructed the hundreds of students that past summer that participated in my clinics. This CPTL match was the first real competitive situation I had been in since I had adopted that instructional point so vehemently. Though the match was a competitive three set battle that was highly entertaining for the spectators, I was profoundly mortified that I couldn't execute the one fundamental I had set out to enforce: "Eyes on contact." At best, I felt I was visually connected to contact point less than thirty percent of the time. Before I left the competitive arena that night, I sat in my car frustrated, devastated, but immensely intrigued. The moment in my car turned into over an hour. I began to realize that the fundamental of "eyes on contact," was not a physical exercise but 100% mental. I was no different than the hundreds of students I had taught, making them aware of their short comings. I lost the match and was swept up in the winds of frustration only to stumble on the greatest epiphany of my life in relation to tennis and sport: WE ARE TWO SELVES.

Chapter

2 **WO**

A Conversation with Dr. Baird

Roger Federer's ability to watch contact point every shot he hits throughout every match he plays is a rare and unique skill. However, it is less fascinating than the visual control he maintains post contact. I was exploring this point with an 85 year old doctor I frequently teach when he is in town. Dr. Baird is in love with playing the game of tennis and has a thirst for learning and improving that is second to none. Many of our lessons would conclude with small successes reached which he would see as giant milestones. Upon occasion, I would think to myself, who got more out of some of our lessons due to some of our lengthy philosophical discussion points that all centered on the game of tennis. Following my CPTL match, Dr. Baird came for a lesson. After a short warm up I told him that most of his unforced errors were due to his eyes shifting off contact point prior to striking the ball. I let my guard down and I told him I had experienced the same problem the night before in my CPTL match even though I had made the conscious effort to stay visually with contact point. I went on to explain that I have had a tennis racquet in my hand since the age of 2 years old and you would think that someone of my experience could, without question, attend to the number one fundamental of any ball sport for at least one match.

I finished detailing my "visual" shortcomings to Dr. Baird and his response was without hesitation and has become the foundation of my philosophy I call **Brain Alignment**. The most important five words that I have ever heard spoken on the tennis court came out of his mouth almost in a whisper as if he were breathing: "YOUR BRAIN IS TOO FAST." My initial response to his comment was flattery. I thought that because of my years of experience on court my brain, specifically, was faster than the average player's brain. However, within seconds of audibly digesting Dr. Baird's comment, I realized the opposite was true. A flood of thoughts rushed through my head as I looked back in bewilderment towards Dr. Baird. All of my students whose inability to have their eyes on contact were no different than me. Each and every one of them had brains that were simply just too fast.

The reason why I could only make my students aware that they were not watching contact, or why I could not stay visually with contact for sustained periods of time was because of the fact I was approaching the instructional point from the wrong angle. As a tennis ball is put in play, there are two major focal points that we experience visually: 1) The tennis ball itself, and 2) everything else. The most important variable on the court is the ball; however, our brains do not allow it to be. Included in the category of *everything else* are the court, the opponent, open space opportunities, closed space, the clouds, the neighboring court distractions, and maybe even a butterfly. The event of ball striking becomes even more convoluted as the moment of contact point approaches. We mentally process the visual *everything else* variables with additional conditions such as the wind, sun, rotation of the ball approaching, your opponent's weapon side, etc., all before we actually decide on our own shot selection. The moment contact point is upon us our eyes are continually compiling empirical data which our brain then processes. The final decision is made to hit a 90 degree change of direction down the line winner and our eyes fixate on the spot, however, contact point has still not been reached. Contact point has been compromised because of a rolling brain trying to process visual data in a panicked state. Remember, it's the ball we're trying to hit as cleanly and uninhibitedly as possible.

The most significant variable that is not empirical in nature is that of trust. Whether we are ball striking off our less natural side, threading the needle, or engaged in a tremendous pressure point in the match, we are primitively predisposition to visually bounce to the point where we anticipate our shot to land versus staying with contact point. Embedded in this trust factor are feelings of hope, fear, uncertainty, and desire. All of these components combined make ball striking a wild ride. We must trust that when we stay with the contact point, the likelihood of hitting a good shot is markedly increased.

Chapter thr3

The Two Selves & Action Commands

The obvious challenge now was for me to find a way to work on slowing down our "fast brain." Dr. Baird's profound comment spawned my philosophy of Brain Alignment. Brain Alignment operates on the theory that in a competitive arena, such as tennis, we are two selves: **The Logical Self**, and **The Athletic Self**.

The Logical Self is the one currently reading this information. It is rational, thoughtful, and understanding. The Logical Self has time to digest, process, and regurgitate information. Instruction and direction make undeniable sense to the Logical Self. Language and elaborate concepts are all working parts that serve to hydrate the Logical Self's thirst for knowledge. The Logical Self rules the court in most occasions until the ball is put in play.

The Athletic Self, however, is best described as a squirrel reacting when an oncoming car is approaching. This squirrel is reactive, undisciplined, and in a state of panic each time the ball is put in play in a competitive fashion. Once competing begins, the Athletic Self takes over, hence, our more primitive state of mind is left to rule all decision making.

The two selves can be best illustrated through the relationship of a human to their animals. In the following examples the human will represent the Logical Self and their animal will represent the Athletic Self. Special attention should be placed upon the language used by the Logical Self to derive action from the Athletic Self.

Example #1:
An owner holds a stick in his hand and then proceeds to throw it yelling "FETCH!" as he releases the stick. The dog, who was by his side until the release point and command was administered, sprints to the stick, picks it up with his teeth, and races back to his owner dropping it in front of him in hopes of the action repeating itself.

Example #2:
An equestrian sits on her horse and commands her horse to "CANTER!".

The horse proceeds to move in a three step beat fashion until the rider commands, "TROT!" in which case the horse moves in a four count rhythm. In cases where the equestrian wants the horse to slow down from a vigorous sprint, the command "WOAH!" is exclaimed.

Dogs and horses are obviously not born with the ability to understand language as we know it. However, through intense repetition and the use of what I call, **Action Commands**, you can train an animal to perform a very specific action. Through a simple reward system, I can train a dog to run directly to the stick and back to me. In the learning phase, the dog may receive a hearty rub down, a treat of some kind, and audible elation from his owner. These rewards serve to solidify the action as being synonymous with the command. The equine world is no different. A simple "Good Boy!" or a meaningful pat will acknowledge success. The animal is thirsty for positive attention, emotional feedback, and harmony with its owner or caregiver.

In my previous example of the dog who responded to "FETCH!" in a generic fashion by running directly to the stick and directly back to its owner, stick in mouth, we saw that the action command administered resulted in the event executed by the animal. What if I decided that "FETCH!" meant my dog had to run around a tree between him and the stick before he could grab the stick. On his way back an additional orbit of the same tree was in order before dropping the stick in front of me. From day one, I would train this dog with the tree in the mix. No matter where I threw the stick, the dog would have to circumvent the tree on the way to the projected object and back. Now, though the action command "FETCH!" has not changed, the sub layers of its meaning has.

Using the horse analogy once more, I could train a horse to canter using the action command "TROT!," and I could train a horse to trot using the action command "CANTER!," thus, reversing technically and competitively accepted action commands in the horse world. Again, this is an important concept to adopt and uphold because we are exploring how action commands can be the same word, but at times, have different meanings.

These previous illustrations are all based on the relationship of human, Logical Self, to animal, Athletic Self. In an athletic event, such as a tennis point, I can distinguish a parallel relationship between human and animal with us. Because there are two very separate entities, one more evolved than the other, action commands administered by the Logical Self can serve to discipline the actions of the Athletic Self.

In my clinics or private lessons, I would emphasize the importance of "eyes on contact" with why this fundamental carries so much weight. As I walk over the net to the students' side of the court, I begin embellishing the action command "CONTACT!" with its voluminous sub layers of information:

The most important fundamental in tennis is eyes on contact and holding them there post contact point. Raising the eyes to see where our shot might land prior to striking the ball has profound negative physical implications that can only serve to compromise our ball striking ability. Holding our eyes through contact yields balance. Balance yields swing stability which, in turn, gives our stroke the greatest potential for success. As we lift our eyes to see our shot (or our minds' preconceived notion of our shot) we also lift our head. When the head is raised so is the torso which then affects our swing plane. A kink in the kinetic chain is experienced when the energy from the ground running up through the power points of the body is derailed because the brain, then eyes, then body left the point of contact prior to contact. Everyone will stop their accelerated brains by saying the word "CONTACT!" at their perceived contact point. The object is to truly be mentally and physically connected to contact point. This audible cue, "CONTACT!," allows for you to truly be "in the moment" as the ball is struck.

A correlation can be drawn here between being *in the moment* as the ball is struck and the practice of yoga. As exercises in the discipline of yoga promote control of the body and mind, the action command "CONTACT!" encourages the player to be mentally and physically connected to the point. In so doing the player maintains his own body and mind control. In the endeavor to gain control of the player's mind and body using cue words or phrases such as "CONTACT!" the player is employing tactics practiced in the Hindu discipline.

The difference between my Peak Season instruction and post Dr. Baird instruction was the action command "CONTACT!" Though, I wouldn't divulge the long winded philosophy of Logical Self vs. Athletic Self, I would empower their Logical Self with the action command "CONTACT!" to their Athletic Self without their knowledge of who either was. All my students knew was to say a word at the moment of contact. The meaning, or sub layers of information had been shed as to the importance of the technique, all they had to do was annunciate "CONTACT!" One after the other would say "CONTACT!" and their eyes would be fixated on contact point and after contact they remained there. Through this action command, I had effectively slowed their brains down to properly execute, finish, and own this athletic event. The most important thing to these students became saying "CONTACT!" at contact point because of the implications of what the sub layers of information "CONTACT!" carried.

In my previous examples about training the dogs and horses to perform on their respective commands, an integral part of the process was the reward mechanism. The animals learn to equate success with physical affection, positive audible cues, or edible treats. They experience success based on external affirmation. We experience our rewards system on a much different level, that of internal affirmation. The action command "CONTACT!" is verbalized by the Logical Self to unite the mind, body, and spirit at the moment of contact point. If executed properly, there is a feeling at contact point that is specific, unique, and unparalleled. In our sport of tennis, we call this perfect ball striking feeling "clean." The feeling of a clean struck ball is undeniable and what we all chase. Our rewards system is based on that quality of feel.

When we feel what is right we become more in tune to the components that got us there. Repeating the mental progression, in a specific sense, to realize the reward, shot in and shot out, must become the foundation of this game. Anything shorter will make us less effective as students and competitors in the game of tennis. Once a feel is established, we cannot guarantee that it will be actualized every time the ball is struck on a consistent basis. However, the mental progression can be consistent, giving the student the best chance possible of repeating the feeling. It is essential to understand that we must chase the process to the reward. The reward in and of itself is a byproduct of the process.

Illustration #1: The Process to Reward

Logical Self mentally digests sub layers of information

Logical Self forms an action command
and sends it to Athletic Self

Athletic Self uses the action command to slow down the brain
and all potential distractions prior to execution

Athletic Self fixates on performing the action command
throughout the course of the physical event

Reward is realized upon completion of the athletic event

Chapter 4our

**The Three F's:
Feet, Focus & Feel**

In my quest to further simplify the inherent complexities of our sport of tennis, I discovered that I could compartmentalize virtually all action commands into three categories respectively. I call these categories the **Three F's** in tennis. They are as follows: **Feet, Focus,** and **Feel.** The Three F's allow us to catalogue and then reference our action commands with ease. It represents an easy middle ground in between the Logical Self and the Athletic Self that both can equally understand and access.

The first category of my Three F's, **Feet,** delineates any action command that has movement implications. I may administer the action command "PREPARE!" to a student who I am working with to get to the location of contact point balanced and loaded prior to striking the ball versus the tendency that students might show to get to the location of contact point as they were hitting the ball. "BALANCE!" might be another solid action command for the same issue. I tend to use "PREPARE!" when working with students on lateral movement structures and "BALANCE!" when working on linear movement planes.

Feet also catalogue movement after point of contact has been made. The action command, "RECOVER!" is typically utilized when stressing the importance of finding the neutral zone or middle of play from a positioning standpoint at the baseline. Many students lack the sense of urgency to find the center of play post contact. After contact has been made, the Athletic Self collects visual data concerning the success, or lack of, the shot. This moment freezes the natural physical process of movement. If an issue, movement must be addressed prior to playing a point or hitting our shots. "RECOVER!" sent from Logical Self to Athletic Self prior to the athletic event enables movement post contact point. The Logical Self is able to override Athletic Self's data collection point by making movement off of contact the focal point.

The action command, "RECOVER!" is used predominantly for baseline play or movement structures that are lateral in nature immediately following contact point. "POSITION!" becomes the action command when on court movement becomes linear or vertical. As we move forward, after we have made contact, the number one objective should be finding proper court positioning in a balanced manner. Whether we are drawn in through our own decision making or we are forced in against our will due to a drop shot or other unscripted short ball, proper court positioning must become a huge priority on the mental and physical level. I will talk about court positioning in further detail as we move forward but understanding the immediate significance of movement post contact and distinguishing a mental separation between linear and lateral movement is of the upmost importance. The following tree depicts the complexity of Feet our first of The Three F's.

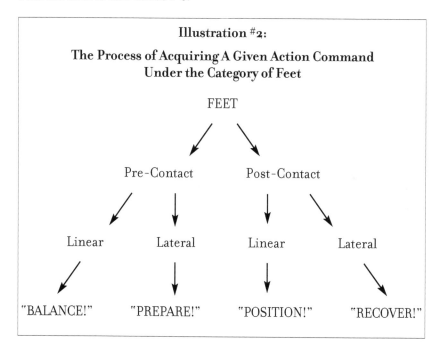

Illustration #2:

The Process of Acquiring A Given Action Command Under the Category of Feet

FEET

Pre-Contact   Post-Contact

Linear   Lateral   Linear   Lateral

"BALANCE!"   "PREPARE!"   "POSITION!"   "RECOVER!"

Remember, these action commands that lie as the foundation of this pyramid, each carries an infinite amount of information. Just as "FETCH!" could mean different things to the dog based on how I trained him to understand the meaning, so could these action commands. In fact, over time, the same action command can evolve and hopefully will to carry different skill sets of information as we evolve as tennis players. For instance, I might work with Player A on his jab step, a footwork technique used upon finishing the service motion to explosively regain balance behind the baseline. Player B already has a functional jab step that was refined months ago and we have moved on to an explosive crossover step after being pulled out wide to properly make it back into play. In both Player A's and Player B's cases I am using the action command "RECOVER!" each carrying its own significant sub layers of information. The action commands will not change although its context will. What one student uses the Action Command to accomplish may be different from what another student uses the same Action Command to accomplish.

The Three F's: Feet, Focus, Feel

The second of my Three F's categories which serves to catalogue a genre of action commands, is **Focus**. This category carries both concrete and more abstract points of reference. Focus implies the specific, such as the visual implications of "eyes on contact." It also covers the broad realm of strategy based principals, such as, in the liberal sense, aggressive or passive styles of point construction. I find the three most common reasons a player is visually disconnected from contact point are as follows:

1) Too much time, too much court

2) Too little time, too little court

3) Hitting the ball off balance or off of our less natural side

The first instance references an opportunity ball every player has encountered at some point in virtually every match they play. The shot that seems to slow time down where the "roll-a-deck" of options A through Z flies through the competitor's brain prior to striking the ball. It is the shot hit from our opponents that carry no pace and contain significant trajectory. Our brains, then eyes, dart from one option to the next where the most important element, contact, is never realized. The comment that Dr. Baird made, "Your brain is too fast!" is acknowledged by all of my students as their most common mistake.

26

The second reason as to why players remove their eyes from contact point relates to being rushed with a specific target to thread. Imagine playing a doubles match against two physically imposing and aggressive net rushers who hit the ball with tremendous pace. The natural instinct is to become visually detached from contact point due to the storming net rushing doubles team. A competitor's eyes will most instinctively look for space or a safe harbor to hit their shot versus fixating on contact point.

Finally, the third situation where contact point becomes a secondary focus is when a competitor is hitting off balance or off of their less natural side. Both of these scenarios contain trust implications which cause our brains, then eyes, to jump to the projected conclusion before the beginning was ever acknowledged. The tennis player's impulse is to visually jerk their attention to the desired outcome. Doubt manipulates and steers the tennis player's thoughts and vision, on the instinctive level, towards a desired end versus engaging thoroughly throughout the process of contact point.

In the specific sense, the action command "CONTACT!" is used, as I described earlier, to suggest being truly "in the moment" at contact point. Using "CONTACT!" at contact point, or where we perceive it to be, unites the mind, body, and spirit. This eliminates any potential set of distractions from what is fundamentally most important.

Where the action command "CONTACT!" deals with the micro or a specific moment, the action command "ENFORCE!" works with the macro, a system of point play. As the level of ball striking, movement and general knowledge of the game of tennis improves we begin implementation of a set of strategies that are designed to give us the best chance of winning.

The classic counterpuncher, an opponent who possesses a style of play that exists on every level, is a great example to illustrate how the category Focus and the action command "ENFORCE!" will give a player the best chance of being mentally and physically balanced throughout the course of a match. The counterpuncher is extremely fast and utilizes his movement capabilities to absorb and reflect pace systematically until his opponent makes an unforced error. He has the mental resilience to weather the storm of big shot making and winners hit against him, knowing that in the end, the opponent will fail due to unforced errors outweighing winners. Coaching against the consistent counterpuncher is one of the greatest challenges in this level of tennis. It requires a firm and specific game plan that tests the patience level of the student to the highest degree.

Properly identifying an opponent's weapons or strengths is the first step in formulating an effective game plan. In this case, the classic counterpuncher's most effective tool is his legs. His quickness and agility around the court allows him to play a consistent game, thus, forcing his opponent into impatient decision making. This results in a slew of unforced errors as the match progresses. Winning against the counterpuncher requires successfully disabling their weapon. When encountering a counterpuncher I coach my students to pin them into a corner with their shot selection. Through an onslaught of penetrating heavy shot making two things happen: 1) The counterpuncher remains relatively in the same spot on the court so predictable angles of opportunity arise, and 2) the open court can be attacked when the shorter opportunity ball has been generated, thus, effectively taking time away from the counterpuncher, thereby forcing them into off balance shot making. Once the game plan has been discussed and the sub layers of information have been processed the action command "ENFORCE!" can be administered.

The dialogue between the Logical Self and the Athletic Self must take place before every point. Turning off the communication line results in the Athletic Self taking over all decision making. It is a tremendous mental challenge to "ENFORCE!" a concrete game plan, point in and point out, for an entire match especially against a counterpuncher, as discussed earlier. It is not uncommon for these matches to run for three or four hours. The mental focus is tested as much as the physical exertion is pushed.

In pre-match interviews concerning upcoming opponents, we often hear the pros explain, "In order for me to be successful today, I must execute my game plan." This comment, though simple in nature, is a complex web of mental, emotional, and physical factors. There are three components to successfully executing a game plan and they are as follows: 1) Devising the right game plan through careful consideration of an opponents' strengths and weaknesses, 2) "ENFORCE!" the game plan prior to playing each point (this is where the action command is administered), and 3) Execute the game plan, which houses the only physical factor of the three components. Through this trinity of "executing a game plan," we understand two parts are mental and one part is physical.

There is an extremely significant element to the **Focus** category, of my Three F's, that cannot be overlooked. A full proof game plan married with world class skill sets will fall prey to emotional imbalance. Controlling the emotional highs and lows within a tennis match, deserves the same attention as being in the moment at the point of contact or working on executing a flawless game plan. Immediately following a point you may experience any feeling covering the emotional spectrum from intense rage and disappointment to a powerful concentration of euphoria and elation. Each emotional reaction is wired directly to a physiological response. For instance, a thirty ball rally ending with a "sitter" overhead hitting the fence could give rise to anger. This emotional interpretation, if let loose, will influence the physiological response with that of tension. A tense body derived from frustration often leads to rash judgment and forcing shot selection in an effort, on the subconscious level, to bring the emotional situation back to a neutral playing field. Too often, playing and competing empowers our emotional fragility and leads to loosing the competitive edge in a tennis match.

When I am working with my students on harnessing their emotional station, I use the action command "CHECK!" In my opinion, this is by far the most complicated set of actions to govern in the game of tennis. It allows the Athletic Self to collect a myriad of emotional data, in an existentialist fashion, before sending the information to the Logical Self. The player must acknowledge their immediate emotional response to the result in the point as well as how they perceive their opponent's reaction. Typically, the immediate emotion set, following a point, between our experience and our opponent's experience are in opposition of one another. After this emotional information is collected it is sent to the Logical Self, where without hesitation the action command "CHECK!" is administered.

Throughout my years of training at the highest levels, I was fortunate enough to be exposed to several sports psychologists who were highly revered in the tennis community. One mental exercise stands out above all others when dealing with my action command "CHECK!" The sports psychologist turned the light off in the room and instructed us to go to a place where we felt most relaxed. A place where the world could not touch you, thus, distancing yourself from stressors and complication. I immediately found myself mentally at the ocean, on the beach, at sunset. The horizon was to the left as I stared at a piece of driftwood before me. I was engulfed in feeling. I could feel the plush sand beneath me, hear the soft waves crashing and receding, and sense the delicate but constant breeze palpitating my body. After giving us five minutes to find our mental tranquility, the sports psychologist reentered the mix. He took us from our entranced state and told us that during emotional anguish in a tennis match we should visit our special state of serenity.

The only problem with this exercise was implementation in match play. I was able to find this sense of calm in a relaxed state; however, I did not possess the mental or emotional skills to find it in the heat of battle. As I delved deeper into the relationship between the Logical Self and the Athletic Self, I remembered my ocean front mental experience. I began working with the concept of how an action command could invoke the spirit of tranquility.

"CHECK!" is the action command used on a point by point basis to bring the emotional condition to a position of calm so the Logical Self can be centered as it communicates its next action command to the Athletic Self. "CHECK!" embodies my beach front landscape and harvests the information collected on the emotional level post point by the

Athletic Self. The emotional repercussions experienced post point has a place where they become diluted to the point of small objects. These objects are important elements as the Logical Self processes what has just transpired and what is to transpire. The emotional arena in tennis and all sports is the most grey. In the game of tennis, placing an action command to the area that is least tangible is extremely significant to personal growth in our sport.

The competitive spirit an individual plays with is deeply embedded in their constitution. A winning nature or a strong competitive drive is something we cannot see, touch, taste, hear, or smell. We can all recall people or performances we have seen in the past, such as Roger Federer or Pete Sampras, who seem to have a competitive edge on the majority of their opponents. Within the greatest pressure points in their match play, time and again, they come up with spectacular successes.

On an individual level, the most awesome display of the competitive winning spirit was illustrated through a dramatic five set match in the Men's Singles Quarterfinals of the 1996 U.S. Open. Pete Sampras worked his magic to beat Alex Corretja in a four hour and nine minute battle with the final score being 7-6, 5-7, 5-7, 6-4, 7-6. In the final tiebreaker of the phenomenal match, Pete, suffering from extreme dehydration, proceeded to vomit at 1-1. Between each point he wilted and held himself up by leaning on his racquet with both hands. At 6-7, match point down, Pete serves and moves forward. Corretja hits an amazing return down low at Pete's feet which he half volleys cross court sending his opponent on the dead run. Corretja gets there balanced and rips a cross court passing shot. Pete lunges to his right with the explosive agility of a cat blocking the passing shot for a stab volley winner. Tied now 7-7 in the final tiebreaker of the match, the circumstances leading up to this point turned the moment into a pressure cooker. After missing his first serve, Pete ambled back to the baseline exhausted. He bent over once more before he addressed his second serve. Pete took a chance with the second serve and aced Corretja out wide. Alex Corretja, now down 7-8 but serving, realizes the moment of utter despair as he double faults giving Sampras the amazing victory.

In my lifetime, sampling a cross section of all sport, this is one of the greatest moments of the winning spirit exemplified. Physically, emotionally, and mentally depleted, Sampras was able to call upon some inner force to come up with a nearly impossible stretch volley match point down and a second serve ace giving him match point. Whether it is a famously documented father-child upbringing such as Andre Agassi or the William Sister's experienced, or the coach-student relationship that Pete Sampras grew from, the inexorable will to win was fostered, cultivated, and fed to a point that nothing could stand in its way.

The winning spirit, without question, lies in us all; however, it exists in varying degrees. Too often, any level of distraction, both specific and general in nature, can inhibit the desire to win or compete. In the prior example of Pete Sampras' unbelievable quarterfinal experience, he had a set of distractions that bombarded him on every level. Something inside of him sparked determination and true grit driving him past the near debilitating set of distractions and on to victory. Most people are not designed inherently to have this winning spirit emerge on reflex. However, through the action command "WIN!" we possess the ability to call on it.

"WIN!" invokes desire and intense determination, the intangibles that constitute the winning spirit. I have discovered that the action command "WIN!" compels us to play with purpose. Competing with purpose yields the best chance of a successful result. The Logical Self must recognize the Athletic Self's vulnerability to distraction and its potential to sabotage the winning spirit. The first step in summoning the competitive drive is acknowledging the distraction or distraction set. The Logical Self must sense the mental imbalance and immediately identify the source. For example, the wind, the sun, fatigue, the court presence of my 6'5" 230 lbs. opponent could be distractions that inhibit the competitive process. Once the source of the distraction is realized, the Logical Self must process the information and catalogue it, then administer the action command "WIN!," thus, deriving a hyper focus on the winning spirit.

The concept of cataloging let alone embracing, a distraction or distraction set sounds counter intuitive by design. While playing for Clemson University, under the tutelage of Head Men's Tennis Coach, Chuck Kriese, I was first introduced to the significance of **recall buttons**. Recall buttons are the foundation of experience. In its fundamental sense, it is the ability to download an experience or a set of circumstances into our memory bank which can be accessed, with a label, by the Logical Self. For example, a universal recall button that we all have encountered at some point in our playing careers is losing a significant lead while trying to close out a match. Though, the experience is negative in nature, it is of vital importance to dissect every aspect of it. Three questions must be asked when formulating a recall button and they are as follows:

1) What was the situation?
2) What was my emotional response before, during, and after the event?
3) How would I handle the situation differently in the future if posed with a similar set of circumstances?

These questions and their respective answers properly identify a situation and catalogue it with a label to be accessed when a similar future event arises.

Recall buttons help feed confidence to the winning spirit. If I have experienced a situation before and I find myself in it again, I have confidence in my ability to handle and manage it in a much more serene level. This sense of ease can only come through working with an experience on a mental level and putting it in a place that the Logical Self can then harvest upon command. As a student of the game, an instructor, and a competitor I find growth in the sport of tennis is based on how we process the collective sum of our experiences. Our experiences can be negative, neutral, or positive in nature, however, embracing them and working with each one on an intellectual level will give us the ability to draw on them when future and similar situations present themselves. Recall buttons are vital ingredients in disseminating distractions in the game of tennis.

The final F of my Three F's categories is **Feel**. Feel is much more specific, than the abstract qualities Focus possesses and the elaborate movement schematics of Feet. Where Focus deals with the visual and mental components, and Feet works with movement based characteristics, Feel addresses swing and stroke production issues. Through technical analysis and, ultimately, the physical implementation of swing aesthetics the most important element of ball striking, Feel, is lost. The concept of Feel creates symmetry between technical instruction and perceived feel.

The topspin forehand, from a technical standpoint, creates the greatest opposition between instruction and feel. One of the fundamental misconceptions of how to hit topspin is that the racquet must travel over the ball. This could not be further from physical fact. The racquet face, at impact, is actually "square" or perpendicular to the ground. The racquet should travel in a windshield wiper motion across your body with the wrist being the catalyst of racquet head speed. Contact is somewhere between the beginning of the wrist snap and the end of the wrist snap depending on the height in which contact is addressed. The racquet face may break to a closed position but it is typically well after contact. Energy from the ground up is transferred through contact which gives the ball various degrees of velocity, rpm, mph, and trajectory.

The sub layers of information embedded within hitting a successful topspin forehand shot are broken down into an array of technical instructional points. These include, but are not limited to, the beginning of the swing plane, the angle of the racquet face at contact point, the direction of the wrist snap, and finally the completion of the swing. The challenge for the instructor is to get the student to feel these technical pieces in one comprehensive swing event.

One great teaching trick that I use to enable stroke production that produces topspin is getting my students to roll the ball over the net, literally. I have them line up as if they were addressing a forehand with contact point being three quarters of the way up the vertical center net strap. I instruct the student to pin the ball in between the net strap and the sweet spot of their racquet and hold it there. I then tell them to try to get it over the net. Each student processes this request in a different manner, but most angle the racquet face in an open fashion and try to scoop it over. At this point, I place the ball in between the net strap and their racquet face and grab their hand that is holding the racquet. The "light bulb" moment arrives when I manipulate their swing plane in a windshield wiper motion across their body. The ball proceeds to roll over the net with topspin. More importantly, they felt it. As soon as a student can equate success with a feeling, they are on the right path.

Before I feed the student their first ball after they discover this feeling, I label it. "FINISH!" is the action command I use for most swing related issues. "FINISH!" enables the swing motion to be one athletic event centered on discovering feel in contrast to a choppy swing plane interrupted by myriad instructional checkpoints. The Logical Self, when speaking in terms of swing related issues, must also have the ability to process, catalogue, reference, and administer feel. If we leave it up to the Athletic Self to figure out the correct swing, especially in the competitive arenas, we will see our old friend the squirrel emerge in a heightened panicked state. Remember the path to discovery, was my ability as the instructor, to keep the Logical and Athletic Self apart until it was time for them to connect in the appropriate manner. The Athletic Self was able to put into feeling the sub layers of technical instruction, which I administered to the Logical Self, when I manipulated the student's swing plane at the net. As the feeling continues to resonate in the Athletic Self, it is up to the Logical Self to begin processing it. I produce the action command "FINISH!" for them so they can better assimilate a feeling with an action command. The Logical Self, at this point, is welcome to attack the production of the feeling with Why's, How's, Where's, and What's, so ultimate understanding is ascertained and then transmitted in the action command "FINISH!"

In summary, The Three F's serve as constants and mental cornerstones that house action commands. As the game of tennis evolves and we improve, gaining a greater knowledge base and physical acumen, Feet, Focus, and Feel remain the same. The set of action commands that I have referenced are also unchanging fixtures. However, the information set that comprise to form an action command is what is constantly evolving. It is also important to note the action commands that I use possess great inherent meaning to me, thus, it is of the upmost significance to consider action commands that provide this same level of meaning to you. For example, I have been working with my six year old son on his tennis game since he could walk. He doesn't understand action commands on a cognitive level as I have discussed them, however, he does know who Batman is. Instead of using "PREPARE!" when alluding to lateral preparation of a groundstroke, I coach him to get to the ball with enough time to say "I'm Batman!" If he does this successfully, he has adequate time to load and then strike the ball. This is the same way I would reference "PREPARE!" to someone older where the term has had time to age and is imbedded in their vernacular fortified with experience.

Chapter 5ive

Comfort Zones Depicted Through Serving & Moving Forward

this chapter's
approach

- Playing tennis on auto pilot
- The five components of serving and moving forward
- The hidden triangle

The dichotomy of the Logical Self and the Athletic Self existing within our brain is most clearly demonstrated through the concept of **comfort zones.** A comfort zone is the Athletic Self's instinctive and emotive based physical response to any set of internal or external stimuli. In my experience as an instructor and coach, I find the greatest sum of a lesson, clinic, or competitive situation for my students are performed on **auto pilot.** It takes a tremendous amount of mental fortitude for the Logical Self to stay engaged on a point in and point out basis. The consistency of an open communication line between the Logical Self and the Athletic Self is a daunting and unnatural task in and of itself. The term auto pilot refers to the Athletic Self taking over any physical endeavor, whether in the practice or the competitive modes. When the Logical Self has effectively checked out of the equation, the Athletic Self is left to run on auto pilot where comfort zones are realized.

The Athletic Self, on auto pilot, and left to its own devices is naked and extremely vulnerable to the intensity of whatever emotion is currently present. Every action truly has an emotional reaction which the Athletic Self responds to on a physiological level. Intense pressure yields panic, elation invokes euphoria, anger issues frustration, and confidence or lack thereof has a measureable behavioral reply. The highest level of tennis is experienced, on a relative scale, when an emotional response is recognized but does not influence the physical condition. The Logical Self must intervene and absorb all emotion. This mental action disrupts Athletic Self's auto pilot and serves to promote the appropriate physical response.

One of the most challenging skills sets in the game of tennis for the instructor to teach and the student to execute is the action of serving and moving forward. I have recently abandoned the traditional terminology of *serving and volleying* and replaced it with *serving and moving forward.* Serving and volleying implies that after we complete the service motion we must take the next ball out of the air. The term, in and of itself, suggests hitting a specific stroke, the volley, after finishing a previous stroke, the serve. No mention is made of how we get to the volley. The Athletic Self's most natural physical interpretation of serving and volleying is an Olympic style dash covering the 18 feet of space between the baseline and the service line in an attempt to intercept the return of serve out of the air. Once the volley is made, harnessing momentum becomes a huge issue as we lose court positioning and balance. The Athletic Self cannot be left on its own, to fend for itself, especially when employing the serving and volleying (or serving and moving forward) skills set. The result of the Athletic Self on auto pilot is chaos.

Serving and moving forward suggests that upon completion of the serve there are movement implications. If we are balanced and calm when addressing contact anywhere on the court we have the best chance possible of quality ball striking whether we are hitting a volley or taking the ball off the bounce as a half volley. The only way I have found to successfully generate this balance and calm approach to moving forward is by administering the action command "BALANCE!" Remember, in the Feet category "BALANCE!" refers to pre-contact linear movement.

I was first introduced to a concept that would later fuel my theories of movement, in the game of tennis. I was at a Country-Western Bar located in Greenville, South Carolina at my Head Pro's bachelor party. I can have a great time anywhere, but a Country-Western venue would never be my first or seventy-sixth place to ever hang out. Much to my surprise, I had an awesome time and at 1:00a.m., I witnessed something that I use in virtually every tennis clinic during Peak Season: "The Electric Slide." At 1:00a.m., in Greenville, South Carolina, at a Country-Western bar amidst a bachelor party, not everyone is in their most rationale and productive states of mind. The bar was heavily populated with people in similar conditions. The most amazing thing, then, took place. The house DJ started playing "The Electric Slide." I am one of the only human beings on the planet that doesn't know the dance steps to "The Electric Slide" and I am truly alright with that void in my life. However, the scattered and random assemblage of patrons became one collective heart beat as they moved in unison and rhythm to "The Electric Slide." I found that sound, a beat, a rhythm, and a cadence could be a phenomenal instructional resource for movement patterns on the tennis court.

At some point, those Country-Western bar patrons, who all flooded to the dance floor to the tune of "The Electric Slide" had to learn the appropriate steps on a cognitive level. However, the tune, beat, or music itself became a continuous action command to everyone who knew the dance no matter their present mental condition. I took this information and began formulizing a plan for serving and moving forward. The cadence I use today is "Serve...One...Two...Split!" If everyone who participated in "The Electric Slide" could nail it at 1:00a.m. in a festive environment, with drink in hand, why couldn't my students perform a similar task, clear minded and sober, during the late morning?

I used "The Electric Slide" experience as a reference material to serving and moving forward. The Logical Self has to adopt the rhythm of "Serve...One...Two...Split!" and then convey it to the Athletic Self as "BALANCE!" If the player is moving in a fashion where balance is the priority, they have the greatest chance of making a quality play on the next ball. The reason serving and moving forward is the most challenging skills set to acquire in the game of tennis, in my opinion, is the five key objectives that must all be met each time we engage in a linear progression post serve. A disruption, in any one of the five components, which involve the action of serving and moving forward, result in potential disaster. The following delineates the five elements that comprise serving and moving forward. Each can stand alone, but collectively create one complicated event:

1. The Serve
2. "BALANCE!" or the "One...Two...Split!"
3. Identifying the nature of the return
4. Reacting to the return with a transition shot
5. Acquiring court positioning after the transition shot has been executed

The vast majority of my instructional audience is doubles based play. The concepts that I will elaborate on have the game of doubles in mind. Beginning with the serve, I am going to demonstrate the most problematic areas within each of the five factors that involve serving and moving forward and then present solutions that will enable a player to make this unnatural event a fluid ride.

The most pronounced and prevalent issue, when used as a catalyst for serving and moving forward, is service placement. In virtually every clinic I teach with new students, I hear the comment expressed after they get beaten by an angle return, "Well, I was just trying to get the serve in." Just trying to get the serve in from a right handed player's perspective on the deuce side leaves the server vulnerable to great angles of opportunity from the returner. This fact comes to light when we discuss the biomechanics of the service motion and understand the geometrical options from the returner's perspective. This is based on which side of their body they are striking the ball. A right handed player's forehand swing plane is inherently a right to left motion. If I do not try to manipulate the flight path of the ball on the deuce side it will naturally move in a right to left fashion reflecting the swing itself. A ball that travels with angle yields a return that can also produce angle. Attempting to chase down an angle return is the beginning of disaster for a player trying to serve and move forward successfully. These same points remain consistent for a left handed player serving to the ad side of the court.

The idea in doubles is to make the opponents hit on *our terms*, limiting the amount of options per shot. When we reduce our opponents' options, through proper serve placement, we control the nature of their return, thus, they have to strike the ball on *our terms*. An opponent is hitting on *our terms* when they are forced to make contact with their **inside wing**. The inside wing is a term I devised that defines a side of the body from which your opponent is striking the ball. The inside wing is the side where the ball striking is closest to the center of the court (the left side from the deuce court perspective and the right side from the ad court perspective) whether the opponent is left or right handed. The inside wing breeds very little shot selection from your opponents. This minimizes potential chaos. Conversely, our opponents are hitting on *their terms* if they are ball striking from their **outside wing**. The outside wing is the side furthest from the center of the court (the right side from the deuce court perspective and the left side from the ad court perspective) and the side that can create the greatest amount of shot selection.

Acknowledging the importance of the inside wing and the limited shot selection that side can produce is the first step. However actually placing the ball there is a tricky proposition. Fortunately, there are two successful teaching techniques that I use that, when combined, maximize service placement potential. First, there is a **triangle** that can be utilized for our serves as a target that is hidden in the court. Look at the vertical net strap, located in the center of the net, and look through the net to see where it intersects with the horizontal service line. Then observe the vertical service line (bisecting the two service boxes) from the "T" and visually bring it back to the net strap, there is a triangle that we can use as a hitting point target. This triangle exists on both the deuce and the ad side and the further you serve from the center hash mark on the baseline the larger the triangle gets (see picture #1 and #2 to reference the triangle). After recognizing the target, the second step is actually placing the ball there. One of the best tips I use for generating proper direction on a shot comes through understanding that the racquet face is literally an extension of our palm. Whatever direction our palm is facing through the moment of contact also dictates the angle of our racquet face. A player can best manipulate the flight path of the ball by thinking in terms of extending their palm towards the target line.

Upon showing my students the triangle that the net and the service lines create, the typical reaction is, "Wow! That's so small!" or "How am I supposed to get it in there, that's nearly impossible!" Richard H. Thaler and Cass R. Sunstein published an article in *The New Republic*, Wednesday, April 9th, 2008 putting an interesting spin on how our brains are adept to aiming towards small targets. They write, "In a busy airport restroom used by throngs of travelers each day, the unpleasant effects of bad aim can add up rather quickly. Enter an ingenious economist who worked for Schiphol International Airport in Amsterdam. His idea was to etch an image of a black house fly on to the bowls of the airport's urinals, just to the left of the drain. The result: Spillage declined 80 percent. It turns out that, if you give men a target, they can't help but aim at it." This experiment, though comical, embellishes the significance of the triangle targets in the service box. Instead of "just trying to get the serve in" which yields the returner hitting the ball on *their terms*, use the targets so you can begin the process of serving and moving forward on *our terms*.

The second problematic area, of the five, when discussing serving and moving forward, references the action command "BALANCE!" My experience at the Country-Western Bar in Greenville, South Carolina was the inspiration for concocting the movement rhythm post serves of "One...Two...Split!" When I worked with my students in clinics or private settings on acquiring the rhythm of moving forward after they hit the serve, they got it. Through a little trial and error, they actually learned rather quickly. The average student would have the movement structure down within a five minute time frame; however, the caveat was that there was no one on the other side to return. Our opponent, the returners, represents accountability when in place. As we work on the rhythm embedded in the movement structure of serving and moving forward with no one present on the opposing side to return, there is no form of distraction from movement post serve. We can slow our brains down to the point that the only predominating factors are the serve and the movement structure. Enter a returner on the other side of the net and the entire mental ball game changes.

Executing the serve then "One...Two...Split!" is a function of the Athletic Self responding successfully to the action commands of the Logical Self. In its most natural and reactive state, the Athletic Self will respond to serving and moving forward in one of two ways: 1) It will become the Olympic sprinter and react in panic, or 2) It will freeze and attempt unsuccessfully for Logical Self to collect data with which the Athletic Self can respond. A player must become aware of what their most natural tendency is when serving and moving forward. Once this awareness is realized, the next step is to discipline the reactive nature of our Athletic Self by making a mental commitment to move forward in a balanced fashion. This mental commitment is properly executed through employing the action command "BALANCE!"

The third and fourth issue a player encounters when attempting to serve and move forward is identifying the nature of the return and then playing it. The "Split" in my cadence post serve of "One...Two...Split!" signifies a slight hesitation in the movement structure forward. It is a means of acquiring almost static balance. In theory, at the "Split" position, a player should have the capacity, to move in any direction on equal agility terms.

The most pronounced dispute concerning where a player should acquire their balance point rests in an area of the court known as *no man's land*. No man's land is the region of the tennis court that lies between the baseline and the service line. The dimensions of this territory run 18 feet vertically by 36 feet laterally, thus covering a tremendous amount of space. Virtually every student I have worked with who has received instruction in the past, believes no man's land is a dangerous space on the court that should never be inhabited. In fact, the implications of the terminology itself, no man's land, suggest a piece of property no one should occupy.

My spin on no man's land stands in polar opposition to the predominant belief system most tennis players own. When assessing the nature of the return so the appropriate and most calculated movement structure can be applied, acquiring balance in no man's land is essential. The most important factor in the complicated event of serving and moving forward is collecting balance in the "Split" of "One...Two...Split!" post serve. Again, the "Split" signifies supreme balance. If a tennis player is still attempting to manage balance after they identify the nature of the return, their off-balance will inhibit the quality of movement towards the ball. Thus, they will be directly affecting the nature of contact when ball striking. The perch, which is discovered upon completion of "One...Two...Split!" is located in the middle of no man's land. At this balance point, amidst the center of no man's land, the player must diagnose the nature of the return. In a general sense, at this position in time and balance, only one of three phenomena can take place: 1) the return can be taken out of the air as a volley, 2) the ball can bounce in front of the balanced server who is moving forward and taken as a half volley, and 3) the server's partner can be lobbed giving the server the responsibility to cover it.

There is one action that requires the least amount of challenges from the balanced point in no man's land. That is taking the opponent's return of serve out of the air as a volley. Upon realization that the return can be played as a volley, fluid movement from the balanced position to contact is in order. Conversely, the returns of serve that produce the most issues are the ones where balance is truly recognized. Returns of serve that require the server to stay put in a balanced position and then are played off the bounce as a half volley create the most perplexing set of circumstances. This scenario challenges the inherent nature of the Athletic Self not to panic and charge the moving yellow object. The most successful approach to a low return that is hit hard but lands shallow in the server's court is playing it as a half volley from a static and balanced position. The logistics of handling this particular return require balance in "no man's land" and a modified compact backswing, thus, enabling the server to use the energy of the ball created by the bounce to produce the shot and its resulting direction. The final piece of handling the return off a balanced position is covering your partner's lob. I will elaborate on the system of doubles positioning I subscribe to further, but it is critical to mention that one of the agility points, from the balanced position, is lateral or even angular.

It is important to mention that I do believe strongly in the notion of no man's land. However, I do not believe it exists in transition. The transition element to the event of serving and moving forward is the point where the ball is struck, thus, bisecting the act of serving and then acquiring positioning. In my opinion, no man's land is only realized if a player occupies that zone of the court post transition shot. The final piece to the serving and moving forward process is to properly acquire court position after the transition shot has been made.

Proper court positioning must be acknowledged prior to hitting the serve. If a player mentally neglects court positioning after the transition shot is struck, the Athletic Self will take over once more and find its comfort zone in a panicked state. There are different philosophies concerning doubles positioning. Regardless of which system a player commits themselves, it is imperative that they follow the rules and guidelines pertaining to the movement structures of their adopted positioning methodology. If the desired court position, post transition shot, is not recognized the Athletic Self will take over, breeding chaos. When coaching doubles strategy and doubles positioning, my job is to eliminate chaos on your side of the court and maximize disruption on your opponent's side of the court. Removing chaos in doubles is disciplining the Athletic Self prior to the point, just as I demonstrated within each of the five objectives relating to the serving and moving forward event.

The triangle

Look at the vertical net strap, located in the center of the net, and look through the net to see where it intersects with the horizontal service line. Then observe the vertical service line (bisecting the two service boxes) from the "T" and visually bring it back to the net strap, there is a triangle that we can use as a hitting point target.

The triangle from the server's perspective prior to point

In line with the server's right arm is the center net strap. The piece of the deuce side service box that remains in this picture is the triangle.

Chapter

6ix

Staggered Formation

Before I delve deeply into the movement patterns, shot selection, and court positioning structure of **Staggered Formation** (the system of doubles strategy I abide by) it is important to document the three predominating visual variables that convolute a doubles point. These three variables possess reactive properties that could each negatively stimulate the Athletic Self if it is not preconditioned to structure. The three visual distraction elements in doubles are: 1) the opponents, 2) your partner, and 3) the ball. The purpose of any doubles system is to have a cohesive plan that both you and your partner share. When a doubles team becomes two independent entities not working together as one unit, distractions and chaos ensue. The only variable of the three that should have merit and warrant focus from a doubles team is the ball. If both doubles partners are cognizant of their role based on their current position the opponents and your partner are irrelevant points of focus. I will further shed light on this fact as I begin deconstructing the system of doubles I teach called Staggered Formation.

I was first introduced to Staggered Formation in doubles after my doubles partner and I both signed to play college tennis at Clemson University. We were both seniors in high school in our fall semesters when we made the commitment to play at Clemson. Upon signing, Coach Chuck Kriese elaborated on this method of doubles play and encouraged us to learn it and apply it throughout our last year of junior tennis. Both my partner and I studied Staggered Formation and believed in it with tremendous passion. By the following summer, we were experiencing amazing results. The success we achieved as a doubles team was not so much a direct correlation to the physical improvements in our respective tennis games, but the knowledge base we acquired on how to play the game of doubles. I became immediately sold on the Staggered Formation philosophy of doubles. Because of its simplicity, and discovering that taking care of my role and my partner taking care of his, both premeditated actions, bred success for the team.

The vast majority of the tennis playing population engages in the game of doubles reactively. I would like to think most players have a plan when they step out on to the court. However, I have witnessed those plans evaporate as soon as the first ball is put into play. The foundation of strategies such as hitting to the weaker player or both partners playing back because they fear the lob are too specific in nature and are only relevant during certain scenarios throughout the duration of an entire match. Staggered Formation arms both partners with a knowledge base equipped with court positioning, shot selection, and movement patterns. Regardless of the opponents strengths and weaknesses and what their favorite shot is, Staggered Formation is a proactive style of play that turns the focus inward where execution is the dominating factor.

The most advanced level of Staggered Formation is realized by a doubles team at the net. Staggered Formation describes the alignment a partnership tries to create and hold in place while at the net. The positioning requires one player to be tight in proximity to the net and their partner to be on or near the service line behind them, in the opposite box, no more than three feet away from the "T." The "T" is the intersection of the horizontal and vertical service lines creating the two service boxes on the tennis court. In theory, it leaves no high percentage shot selection option available for the opposing doubles team. I maintain doubles matches are predominantly won on our opponent's unforced errors, not our winners. If the foundation of Staggered Formation is to visually and physically reduce the amount of high percentage shot selection from your opponents, then your team forces them into lower percentage shot selection options. Over time, forcing your opponents into less visual and physical space with their shot selection will breed unforced errors. *Picture #3 and #4 illustrates Staggered Formation.*

I will break down each position on the doubles court in and of itself, thus, describing positioning, shot selection, and movement patterns inherent to each player's location or starting point before the point begins. The four roles I will deconstruct in detail are: 1) Server, 2) Server's partner, 3) Receiver, and 4) Receiver's partner.

Before I begin examining the operations of each position, I must elaborate about the significance of the **first exchange** in doubles. The term, first exchange, traditionally suggests the first two shots exchanged or struck in any given point. A high percentage of all points played in the game of doubles are won or lost due to the ability to execute or failure to execute proper shot selection within the first exchange. I believe within the first exchange a player can visually ascertain their opponent's movement patterns which, ultimately, suggest their initial intentions of acquiring court positioning. This information allows a doubles team to work in unison and play or compete with a greater plan, one that functions on the rules of court positioning. There are only three scenarios in doubles that can take place in the first exchange which give you the information set you need to properly position yourself for the extent of the point.

The three scenarios are:

1. You are the server and can find Staggered Formation through serving and moving forward

2. You are the receiver playing against a server who stays back which will enable the receiver and the receiver's partner to acquire Staggered Formation

3. You are the receiver playing against the server moving forward in which case you will stay back and play defensive formation

Staggered formation with server moving in from the duece side
The Server has acquired positioning a few feet to the right of the "T" while Server's Partner remains close in proximity to the net.

Staggered formation with the server moving in from the ad side
The Server has acquired positioning a few feet to the left of the "T" while Server's Partner remains close in proximity to the net.

Chapter

7even

The Server

Inherently, the Server's side of the doubles court is proactive in nature and the receiver's end is largely reactive. The Server has the ability before every point is played to make the mental commitment to serve and move forward. In the Staggered Formation system of doubles, the server's role is to move forward and acquire court positioning around the service line close in proximity to the "T." The five components that I developed in accordance with serving and moving forward must be employed and executed. The server's shot selection must be directed towards the receiver's inside wing. Remember, your opponent's inside wing yields considerably less shot selection opportunities than their outside wing. Once the Server obtains proper court positioning after the transition shot is played, they are responsible for covering two potential shots from the opponent which ultimately dictates the Server's movement patterns. If the Server is able to place the transition shot into their opponent's inside wing, the potential movement patterns of the Server become extremely specific. All shots played from the Receiver through the center of the court and all lobs become the Server's responsibility. After the server gains proper positioning, and is mentally preconditioned to what their responsibility set includes, both the middle and all lobs hit over the server's partner are within reach of the Server.

There are a couple of tricky shots that are necessary to have in your arsenal to effectively run Staggered Formation. Depending on what side of the court you are maintaining and what hand you play tennis with, a player covers their partner's lob with either an overhead or a high backhand volley. A right handed player who has served and moved forward from the ad side must cover their partner's lob with an overhead. Left handed player faces the same scenario from the deuce side. However, one of the most unnatural shots in the game of tennis is covering your partner's lob with a high backhand volley. This is experienced by a right hander when serving and moving forward from the deuce side and a left hander when they are serving and moving forward from the ad side of the court. I seldom find students I teach to work on this shot regularly if ever. The high backhand volley is not a complicated shot. It is just grossly unnatural. It is a vital component in sustaining the Staggered Formation system. The analogy I use to describe how to hit this shot is to "close the shower curtain." This is a great teaching technique for this shot because when you close a shower curtain you use shoulder, not the wrist or elbow, which is the exact same mechanism employed when trying to hit this abnormal shot.

Very few tennis players possess the ability to generate any significant pace on the high backhand volley, hence, placement is critical. It is imperative to keep this ball away from the opposing net player and direct it towards the returner as a **recovery shot**. A recovery shot in tennis is exercised when a player who is out of position needs to buy time to recover proper court positioning. After the lob recovery shot is played back to the returner high and deep in the opposing court, the server must move to the spot closest in proximity to the net which the Server's partner once inhabited. Once the server's partner has been lobbed they move to occupy the space the server just left on the service line by the "T." The high backhand volley recovery shot allows a shifting of positions to take place, ultimately preserving the Staggered Formation system of doubles.

The two areas within this structure of doubles that spawns the most discussion are:

1. The student's presumption that they do not have ample time to cover the lob

2. Moving back into the position the Server's partner once held is counter intuitive on every level

In defense of the first discussion point, I conducted an experiment where the purpose was to incinerate this myth. I hit one hundred lobs and timed the flight path of the ball beginning at the moment I made contact to the moment the ball bounced on the other side of the court. I positioned myself on the court as the returner and I hit the lob down the line as if I was lobbing over the head of the opposing Server's partner. I placed each lob within a few feet of the opposite baseline and I took the average time of all one hundred lobs hit. On average, it took 2.50 seconds for the ball to travel off my racquet and land on the opposing court. The following week I had a 3.0 ladies group in house participating in tennis clinic instruction. There were twelve ladies in the group and I timed each individually on how fast they could move from the Server's net position in Staggered Formation (on the service line several feet from the "T") to the approximate location of where my one hundred lobs landed (several feet inside the baseline on the singles line). I compiled their times and they produced an average of 1.76 seconds collectively.

The inherent problem with my case study of the timed lobs and then a timed sprint of each lady in my clinic was the fact that it was, in essence, synthetically manufactured. As each lady lined up in the appropriate position, point A, and was told to sprint to a desired and marked target, point B, I become their Logical Self. I engaged their Athletic Self by exclaiming "Go!" Prior to their short sprint (representing court coverage), I explained I would be timing them between these two points of reference and they were to get from Point A to Point B as fast as they could upon the command "Go!" Devoid of this experiment were shots hit, movement to acquire balance, court positioning issues, and most importantly opponents on the other side.

Each one of these factors during point play within a match, in real time, serves to generate focus away from the task at hand, whatever that may be.

The Server must construct a **mental progression** before each point is played which essentially is a dialogue between the Logical Self and the Athletic Self. This mental progression functions as court positioning awareness and the subset of responsibilities that it entails. The questions involved with the mental progression include:

1. Where am I? (as far as court positioning is concerned)
2. What shot selection am I preconditioned to use?
3. What are my court coverage assignments or movement patterns that I must know?

This dialogue or mental progression produces a proactive form of playing the game of doubles. If the Logical Self does not instigate this accountable set from the Athletic Self, there is no movement, court positioning, or shot selection plan. Therefore the player resorts to a very reactive style of play. Doubles, played on the reactive level, will fall prey to the lob most of the time. However, once the mental progression from the server is employed, lob coverage becomes an inherent part of their job responsibilities based on court positioning. With this awareness prior to the ball being put in play, the Server will realize a proactive style of doubles.

The second discussion point that finds its way into every clinic I run as I attempt to breakdown Staggered Formation from the Server's perspective is as follows: After the recovery shot is played, moving back into the position the Server's partner once held is counter intuitive on every level. The natural trend or instinct for the server once they have covered their partner's lob, especially with the high backhand volley, is to stay in their place where they made contact or **sleep walk** back to a comfort zone, which is typically the baseline. I utilize the term sleep walking because the movement off an unnatural shot, such as a high backhand volley, is not based on conscious decision making. Sleep walking is the Athletic Self's attempt to migrate into an area of the court where it perceives it has the most time to react. This movement pattern, however, ultimately exposes the center of the server's side of the court and promotes chaos for the extent of the point.

The movement pattern performed off a recovery shot the Server plays is the direction back to the position the Server's partner once held. I call this movement structure, post shot played, **dynamic court positioning**. In contrast, **static court positioning** is the server staying put or sleep walking back to a comfort zone after the recovery shot is played. There are three reasons dynamic court positioning is significant, they are:

1. The Server creates a visual distraction to the receiving side
2. The middle of the Server's side becomes less and less of an opportunity to hit through with every step forward the Server takes
3. Staggered Formation is realized once more by the doubles team

There is absolutely no question that hitting a high backhand volley as a recovery shot, then moving forward to acquire tight net positioning is very unnatural. Because of this, I drill my students through every clinic I teach making this integral part of the Server's responsibility a fluid action. Without repetition and a clear comprehension of this position and movement structure, the Athletic Self will be left to roam in a highly reactive state.

The high backhand volley is used by the Server as a recovery shot. However, when covering your partner's lob with an overhead the scenario slightly changes. The overhead is executed from the right hander's perspective when the server begins the point from the ad court and the left hander will cover their partner's lob with an overhead from the deuce court. Unlike the high backhand volley, the overhead can often times be an effective finishing shot. If the server realizes balance and believes they can finish the point with a powerful overhead, ball placement should be cross court hit towards the player closest in proximity to contact. This is the receiver's partner at the net. Conversely, if the server does not have the means to acquire balance and hit a penetrating finishing shot, then the overhead should be played as a recovery shot down the line to the receiver. In either case, similar court positioning is ascertained, once the overhead has been played to that of covering the lob with a high backhand volley. Thus, dynamic court positioning is enforced and regenerating the tight net position once held by the Server's partner becomes the priority. In such an event the structure of Staggered Formation is maintained. *Pictures #5, #6, and #7 illustrate lob coverage with a high backhand volley and then recovering position at the net and pictures #8 and #9 illustrate lob coverage with an overhead.*

Identifying the lob as one of the responsibility sets for the server
The Server is moving to cover his partner's lob.

Closing the shower curtain
The analogy I use to describe how to hit this shot is to "close the shower curtain." This is a great teaching technique for this shot because when you close a shower curtain you use shoulder, not the wrist or elbow, which is the exact same mechanism employed when trying to hit this abnormal shot.

Dynamic court positioning

The high backhand recovery shot has been hit and now the Server is recovering back to the tight net positioning. The movement pattern performed off a recovery shot the Server plays is the direction back to the position the Server's partner once held. I call this movement structure, post shot played, dynamic court positioning.

The server identifies a lob
and begins positioning himself for the overhead

The overhead is executed from the right hander's perspective when the server begins the point from the ad court and the left hander will cover their partner's lob with an overhead from the deuce court.

Acquiring proper position to strike the overhead

Unlike the high backhand volley, the overhead can often times be an effective finishing shot. If the server realizes balance and believes they can finish the point with a powerful overhead, ball placement should be cross court hit towards the player closest in proximity to contact. This is the receiver's partner at the net. Conversely, if the server does not have the means to acquire balance and hit a penetrating finishing shot, then the overhead should be played as a recovery shot down the line to the receiver.

Picture 9

Chapter

8ight

The Server's Partner

this chapter's
approach

- Movement patterns of the
  Server's partner

- **Outside wing** vs. **Inside wing**

The role of the Server's partner in Staggered Formation carries movement pattern and shot selection responsibilities as well. The same mental progressions the Server engages in prior to playing the point should be experienced by the Server's partner. The Server's partner's movement structure is simple in nature as their assignment is to cover everything left and right of them that is within reach. All lobs that the Server's Partner cannot line up to hit as an overhead, and subsequently finish the point, are deferred to the server. It is the server who possesses the responsibility of lob coverage. If the lob is hit over the Server's Partner's head, he will move diagonally back to occupy the space the Server once held by the "T," on the service line of the neighboring service box. The Server's Partner's shot selection is one dimensional with a very specific intention in mind. He is to direct each volley towards the opponent closest to him - Receiver's partner - with the purpose of ending the point.

There are a set of reactive properties inherent to the Server's Partner's position. However, these elements can be forecast prior to the ball being put in to play. Remember, if the Server is able to place his serve, or any shot after that, to the Receiver's inside wing, it greatly reduces the angle potential of the return. The proactive dynamic of the Server's Partner's position is recognizing if the Receiver is striking the ball with his inside wing or his outside wing. Properly acknowledging the way the Receiver addresses contact will implicate movement on a reactive level. *Pictures #10 and #11 show the Servers Partner's movement patterns based on how the Receiver addresses contact and picture #12 references shot selection.*

The movement patterns of the Server's partner are completely dictated by which wing the receiver is striking the ball. If the receiver is making contact with their outside wing it is imperative that the Server's partner move in the direction of the doubles ally, thus, covering the down the line potential of the return. As the Server's partner slides towards the doubles ally, he visually blocks any opportunity by the receiver to pass the Server's partner down the line from his outside wing. If the Server is able to direct the serve, or any following shot, to the Receiver's inside wing, his angle potential becomes significantly diminished. The Server's partner's job is to *sell* the receiver court positioning information on the visual level. When the Server's partner is able to diagnose ball striking from the inside wing of the receiver, it is of the upmost importance that they do not move towards the center until the receiver commits to his shot selection. Because the Server's partner is *selling* his positioning as visually covering the doubles ally, it will force the receiver into a shot played through the center. As discussed, the inside wing produces little to no angle when hitting the ball back where it came from and away from the Server's partner. Once the receiver has committed to his shot selection, the Server's partner can move towards the center of the court at an angle in the direction of the net to properly cut off the return. Then it can be played as a finishing shot at the opposing net man.

A successfully executed poach requires specific technical components that, left unattended, yield potential chaos. Regardless of being left or right handed, as a player moves towards the center of the court attempting to cut off a return of serve, the biomechanics of the volley stroke, closest to center, naturally extend away from the premeditated target, the opposing net man, and towards the returner. If the Server's partner engages in a poach, and plays the volley in the direction of the inherent nature of the swing, the receiver has an opening down the line which produces a winner, sets the point back to a neutral situation, or breeds chaos from the serving side. Properly directing the poach at the opposing net man suggests formulizing a mental progression prior to the point and physical execution throughout the duration of the poach itself. Generating this inside out direction on the poach volley is derived through hip turn. The angle of the racquet face at contact point should be directed towards the opposing net man. The appropriate means of acquiring this direction is through aligning the hips in the direction of the desired target. This move, in turn, manipulates the angle of the racquet face without the arm acting independently of the core. Once the hips are in line and the angle of the racquet face is set, the player can move towards contact point with full weight transfer traveling in the direction of the poach volley.

In September of 2009, I competed in the Open National Tennis Championships held in Las Vegas, Nevada. My doubles partner, Carlos Lozano, was an All-American doubles player out of BYU and a great friend and colleague. We had played doubles together on many occasions and had phenomenal success. Our styles of play, though drastically opposite from one another, complimented each other as a doubles team. In our first match, Carlos bombed a first serve down the "T" to the inside wing of the receiver. I instantly picked up the direction of the serve and hesitated before moving toward center in the attempt of cutting off the return. As the receiver committed to the direction of the return, I began moving towards the center. The return floated over the center as I had properly anticipated and I stuck the volley. However, I did not consider the direction of my volley prior to the point and instead of placing the poach volley towards the opposing net man, I played it back to the receiver. The corresponding result of my fantastic poach hit in the wrong direction was failure. The returner took my volley back down the line before Carlos or I could even blink.

This experience became an important teaching tool for me that I continue to pass along to all of my students. I have been instructing the Staggered Formation system of doubles for eleven years and competing within its structure for seventeen years. I realized at the conclusion of that point where I misdirected the volley, how important to the process of execution the mental progression is, prior to the point. The human eye and its processor, the brain, would much rather direct the ball into perceived open space then at a target without identifying the mark before the point is played. The mental progression suggests movement and shot selection implications. Failure to acknowledge both results in poor execution.

Server's partner tracking the outside wing of the receiver
If the receiver is making contact with their outside wing it is imperative that the Server's partner move in the direction of the doubles ally, thus, covering the down the line potential of the return. As the Server's partner slides towards the doubles ally, he visually blocks any opportunity by the receiver to pass the Server's partner down the line from his outside wing.

Picture 10

Server's partner tracking the inside wing of the receiver

The inside wing produces little to no angle when hitting the ball back where it came from and away from the Server's partner. Once the receiver has committed to his shot selection, the Server's partner can move towards the center of the court at an angle in the direction of the net to properly cut off the return.

Picture 11

The shot selection of the server's partner

The Server's Partner's shot selection is one dimensional with a very specific intention in mind. He is to direct each volley towards the opponent closest to him - Receiver's partner - with the purpose of ending the point.

Picture 12

Chapter 9ine

The Receiver

The receiving team is fundamentally the more reactive side of the court. However, the direction of the returns and movement pattern plans can be put in place through a series of **If...then** statements prior to the point being played. For instance, a returner might think: "If the server stays back after hitting the serve, then my partner and I will move forward into Staggered Formation." Another example concerning return shot selection is: "If the Server's partner leaves early again in anticipation of a poach volley then I will take the return down the line." These If...then statements, derived from a reactive position, are the receiving teams version of a mental progression. Generating insight based on the serving team's trends establishes a game plan that creates proactive guidelines in a reactive setting.

I believe that virtually all returns of serve should be hit through the middle of the court. The same triangle target, found embedded within the service box using the net strap as the third leg of the triangle, can be visualized from the returner's perspective. When a returner fixates on this target, the server's partner or the server produce very little to no distraction elements making the placement of the return a pure exercise. Perfect execution of a return of serve is not only a ball played back through the center, but more importantly a low ball played back through the center of the serving team. There are two major issues students always seem to bring up in response to returning through the center on a consistent basis. These disputes are:

1. How can I effectively return through the center of the serving team and keep it away from the server's partner?

2. With this consistent return shot selection, don't I run the risk of becoming predictable enabling the server's partner to poach at will?

In response to the first question, I devised a teaching concept I call lining up **outside of the box**. The vast majority of students who have trouble returning away from the server's partner address the return stance in accordance with the geometry of the tennis court. The tennis court is an arrangement of linear lines creating an enormous rectangle with a subset of smaller rectangles and squares. It is most natural for a player to line up, or address a return of serve, using the inherent geometry of the court as a foundation for preparation. However, when a player lines up in this fashion, their core, which is the source of direction, is in a direct line with the server's partner. Any return struck from the inside wing or caught late from the outside wing will travel within the **reach realm** of the server's partner. The reach realm is a term I devised to describe the perceived distance the server's partner will move to intercept a return of serve. A returner who lines up outside of the box faces their core in a direct line with the server. Instead of addressing the return of serve within the geometric structure of the court, the returner is now aligned with the server. The natural swing planes do not change, but by creating this angle, the returner is able to manipulate the direction of his return away from the server's partner. *Picture #13 shows both the Receiver's triangle target and lining up outside the box.*

The second issue concerns the nature of predictability if a returner is consistently directing his return of serve through the center of the serving side. This is completely valid. My immediate response to this question alluding to return strategy is: "Yes, you become very predictable!" However, predictability is not a negative property for several reasons. First, if a returner aims through the center they are returning through the lowest part of the net and the largest area of the court. The center is essentially the highest percentage shot selection in the game of tennis, period. Second, a return through the center nullifies any angle from the server coming in or server's partner poaching across. The serving team playing a return hit through the center has fewer geometric opportunities then a return played down the line or out wide. Finally, doubles is a game not designed to hit away from the opponent. Rather it's a game about controlling court positioning and managing potential chaos through proper shot selection. The returner's predominating philosophy should be to place the burden of shot making back on the serving team through an area of the court that generates little to no angle.

The decision to return serve down the line has to be premeditated and communicated to the returner's partner prior to the point. Remember, the most important variable on the court is neither your partner nor your opponents. It is the tennis ball. If the Athletic Self is left unattended on the return of serve, the slightest flinch from the server's partner can produce enough of a distraction element to dictate the nature of the return. The returner's eye will pick up movement from the server's partner and play shots outside their reach realm. They will often spray the return wide cross court or the returner will try to beat the server's partner down the line which commonly results in net errors. Again, the direction of the return of serve is part of the mental progression a player must go through prior to the point. Alerting the receiver's partner to the fact that the return may be played down the line before the serve is put into play holds the returner accountable for that shot selection. This informs the receiver's partner so they are aware of the possible court positioning implications it might entail.

The final piece of the returner's first exchange event, after the return is played back through the center, is acknowledging the result of the If...then statement internalized prior to the point. The proper diagnosis of this If...then statement reveals court positioning implications for the receiver. The two If...then statements are as follows:

74

1. If the server stays back after their serve has been put in play, then the receiver will move forward with their partner into Staggered Formation at the net

2. If the server moves forward after their serve has been put in play, then the receiver will stay back in a defensive positioning structure

The first If...then scenario suggests the realization of Staggered Formation from the receiving team if the serving team does not move forward and take advantage of their offensive opportunity. This opportunity presents itself to the returner often, but is seldom taken advantage of for many of the same reasons the Server will fail to move forward after hitting the serve in play. The only difference with arriving into Staggered Formation as the receiver versus the server is that the receiver can find this positioning structure more directly and without the transition shot. In fact, the return itself is the vehicle into Staggered Formation and for all intent and purposes acts as the transition shot. The return of serve can be taken inside the baseline and the nature of the shot carries more depth due to the swing plane moving in a low to high fashion. This is in contrast to the service swing which moves downward from contact point to the finish. These two variables constitute less distance to travel to acquire Staggered Formation and slightly more time to get there. Once Staggered Formation is obtained, the same fundamental guidelines of this positioning structure for the Serving team apply to the receiving team. The receiving team has now shifted from defensive court positioning to offensive court positioning by employing the If...then statement prior to the point.

There is a second If...then statement for the receiver to acknowledge prior to the point. If the server moves forward after hitting the serve then the receiver must stay back and adopt the defensive court positioning. The receiver, in this situation, should manage their baseline and exercise **shot tolerance** through the middle of their opponent's side of the court. I propagated the term shot tolerance to represent the receiver's ability to stay steadfast to one target with their shot selection until an outcome or opportunity is realized. Too often, the receiver's Athletic Self is visually distracted by the server's partner at the net and the server moving forward. This visual presence from the serving team creates panic and low percentage shot selection. Again, the power of the If...then statement is appreciated through discipline in court positioning and shot selection through the extent of the point. These If...then statements represent the mental progressions a receiver must engage in prior to the point, thereby allowing the Logical Self to communicate to the Athletic Self. *Pictures #14 and #15 illustrate the movement patterns of the Receiver based on the Server's movement trends post serve.*

Receiver lining up outside the box and the receiver's triangle

A returner who lines up outside of the box faces their core in a direct line with the server. Instead of addressing the return of serve within the geometric structure of the court, the returner is now aligned with the server. The natural swing planes do not change, but by creating this angle, the returner is able to manipulate the direction of his return away from the server's partner. This picture also shows the Receiver's triangle which is much larger than the Server's triangle due to the angle from which the return of serve is addressed.

Picture 13

If the server stays back then the receiver moves forward
If the server stays back after their serve has been put in play, then the
receiver will move forward with their partner into
Staggered Formation at the net.

If the server moves forward then the receiver stays back
If the server moves forward after their serve has been put in play,
then the receiver will stay back in a defensive positioning structure.

Chapter

10en

The Receiver's Partner

this chapter's approach

- Receiving Partner's mental progression
- Shot selection and placement
- **I woulda coulda shoulda moments**

The last position left on the doubles court to discuss is that of the receiver's partner. This position is the most reactive in nature of the four. In fact, it is deemed the "Hot Seat" by those who play and instruct. The receiver's partner cannot engage in the act of ball striking until after the third ball has been played or the progression of the first exchange has been formulized. The mental progression the player in the "Hot Seat" must deliver includes If...then statements that implicate vision line, shot selection, and movement patterns that run continuously throughout the point.

The vision line or visual focal points the receiver's partner must capture prior to the point and during the course of the point serve as cues that dictate proper movement patterns fostering opportunistic court positioning. One of the most significant misconceptions in the game of doubles I find as an instructor is the idea that the receiver's partner must help with calling the serve in or out. In singles, it is the receiver's responsibility alone to make his own line calls and it should be no different in the game of doubles. It is imperative that the receiver's partner fixates on the server's partner at the net prior to the point and through the return of serve until further information is gathered. The server's partner is the first player on the opposing side that can strike the ball after the return of serve is played. Because of this fact, the receiver's partner must visually and physically (literally angle the body in the direction of server's partner) address the server's partner through the serve and a portion of the return. If the eyes of the receiver's partner continually track the flight path of the serve and then the return, they will never pick up on potential movement, or lack thereof, from the server's partner. It is essential in the game of doubles to physically and visually align yourself with the position on the opposing side that can first hit the ball.

The following If...then statements represent the mental progression the receiver's partner must acknowledge prior to playing the point. This begins with a proactive constant:

1. The receiver's partner must visually and physically address the server's partner to collect information which dictates court positioning

2. If the server's partner moves to poach the return of serve, then receiver's partner must manage their current position ready to react in a defensive fashion

3. If the return of serve bypasses the server's partner, then the receiver's partner must turn their visual and physical attention towards the server

4. If the return of serve bypasses the server's partner and the server stays back, then the receiver's partner can move forward to a tight net positioning becoming the front man in Staggered Formation

5. If the return of serve bypasses the server's partner and the server moves forward, then the receiver's partner must interpret the body language and racquet preparation from the oncoming server and use it as information to base their proper court position

6. If the return of serve bypasses the server's partner and the server moves forward erect with his racquet positioned above net level, then the receiver's partner must manage his current position ready to react in a defensive fashion

7. If the return of serve bypasses the server's partner and the server moves forward crouching low with his racquet face net level or below, then the receiver's partner can move forward squeezing the center of the court anticipating a ball played low to high traveling over the center of the court

Pictures #16 through #19 depict various movement patterns by the Receiver's partner based off If...then statements.

The one constant and six If...then statements I alluded to are futile measures if the returner does not attempt to play the return through the center of the court. The proactive nature of the mental progression, no matter what position a player occupies on the doubles court, create job responsibilities that work in accordance with their respective partner's mental progression and corresponding job responsibilities. True chemistry within a doubles team is achieved when each member acknowledges and makes an effort to execute their premeditated set of challenges based on their court positioning.

All of these If...then statements are logic driven and are the high percentage reactive plays for the receiver's partner that support the physics of the game of doubles. The one If...then statement that I want to expand upon is that of moving forward and squeezing the center once the return has bypassed server's partner and the server is playing the volley or half volley net level or below. Failure to move forward on this opportunity produces what I call **I woulda, coulda, shoulda moments** from the receiver's partner's perspective. If the Logical Self does not embark on the mental progression of the If...then statements prior to the point, the action in front of the Athletic Self happens too fast to react with purpose. After an opportunity has been squandered or missed entirely, the Logical Self will dwell on the I woulda, coulda, shoulda moment. The disappointment experienced upon reflection should serve as an informative tool to provoke and inspire future similar opportunities to be capitalized upon and corrected. The only way a player can properly take advantage of such scenarios is by mentally running through the necessary dialogue between the Logical Self and the Athletic Self.

Shot selection for the receiver's partner is very specific in nature. All balls played by the receiver's partner should be directed to server's partner. If the receiver's partner is in a position to strike the ball, it should be placed within the realm of the person with the least amount of reaction time in relation to their position. The other advantage in playing the ball towards the server's partner is that the ball's flight path is moving over the highest percentage region of the court. This is the low part of the net and the big part of the court. All volleys struck by the receiver's partner should be executed with the intent to end the point. If the receiver's partner plays these volleys in the direction of the server chaos will ensue. The server inherently has more time to react and, the down the line option as a response to the misguided volley by the receiver's partner, becomes prevalent.

If the server's partner poaches then receiver's partner stays

If the server's partner moves to poach the return of serve, then receiver's partner must manage their current position ready to react in a defensive fashion.

Picture 16

If the server moves forward and is above the net at contact point then the receiver's partner stays

If the return of serve bypasses the server's partner and the server moves forward, then the receiver's partner must interpret the body language and racquet preparation from the oncoming server and use as information to base their court position. If the return of serve bypasses the server's partner and the server moves forward with his racquet up positioned above net level, then the receiver's partner must manage his current position ready to react defensively.

Picture 17

If the server moves forward and is below the net at contact point, then the receiver's partner closes the net

If the return of serve bypasses the server's partner and the server moves forward crouching low with his racquet net level or below, then the receiver's partner can move forward squeezing the center of the court anticipating a ball played low to high traveling over the center of the court. Here the Receiver's partner sees the Server moving forward and addressing a ball below net level.

Picture 18

Reciver's partner picks off server's half volley

This picture is a continuation of the movement forward in Picture #18.
The Receiver's partner has properly moved forward pinching the center
of the court at the net and is now above net level ready to direct contact
towards the Server's Partner.

Picture 19

Chapter
11 ven
Reactive Analysis

On the doubles court, the purpose of deconstructing each position into a set of specific shot selection guidelines, movement patterns, and court positioning structures is to proactively enforce a game plan. The more experience a tennis player accumulates, the more an analytical presence becomes a part of competing. Too often, tennis players allow **reactive analysis** in terms of what has immediately transpired to dictate decision making concerning shot selection, movement patterns, and court positioning for the corresponding point. Imagine a doubles partnership where both players are engaged on an individual basis, independently analyzing each point, and reacting on their own terms. This trap that many doubles teams fall prey to is quintessentially a recipe for disaster.

The primary teaching objective I employ, when developing doubles teams, is to construct a knowledge base of how each position on the court has a set of responsibilities and guidelines to follow that compliment their partner's position and role. I encourage my students to stick to this knowledge base constituting an overall game plan for their match. It is imperative that regardless of how a team is winning or losing a match they stick to these proactive measures. Any deviations in this game plan due to the analytical and reactive accommodations yields squandering and stagnation in the process of development. If a game plan is executed but the doubles team experiences a loss, it is usually a result of a diminished skill set embedded within the responsibility structure of a position. For instance, if a doubles team loses to a pair of lobbers, it is not the lobs in and of themselves that win but the failure to cover them properly within the Staggered Formation guidelines that led to the loss. Instead of both players moving back to accommodate their lack of skill, turning the match into a chaotic fiasco, I encourage the doubles team to continue running the Staggered Formation system regardless of the outcome. Losing, while trying to exercise a game plan, carries a tremendous amount of growth potential. Exposing voids or weaknesses within a player's game produces quality information in a specific sense. The idea regarding a player's development is to recognize and improve deficiencies to the point of functionality. This is a constant process that requires attention, resilience, and repetition. The comfortable and easy way out is to avoid a weakness by migrating to areas of the court during competition that allow concealment. Maximizing a player's learning curve in the game of tennis is realized when deficiencies are noted and strategies are put in place to strengthen them.

Having this extensive knowledge base and employing it allows players to compete on the proactive level. Without such a game plan, that conditions the Athletic Self on a point by point basis, tennis players are subject to perform reactively. Competing in a reactive nature breeds chaos. Shot selection, court positioning, and movement patterns are dictated by comfort zones. Most players whose tennis is experienced through the Athletic Self alone lack discipline in these three genres that exist within every point. Recognizing this fact grants tennis players in touch with both the Logical Self and the Athletic Self to manipulate their opponent's decision making. The following example expounds this principle.

I was recently teaching a group of 4.0 ladies and I saw ego personified through a forehand. With it a huge tennis epiphany was realized. I was conducting a live ball doubles drill where I was the server staying back and working on the receiver's side. It was staged that I serve to the center "T" and the receiver was instructed to direct the return of serve down the center and come in behind their shot since the server was staying back. Each of the four ladies in the group got an opportunity to return the points. The last of the ladies came up to return on the ad side. I served the first ball medium paced with no action into her forehand and she proceeded to annihilate the ball. She came in behind the return and I popped up a floater which she crushed for a winner. The next six returns at least equaled if not bettered the first return. On the eighth return something interesting happened, my partner decided to poach. The return, again, exploded off her racquet but this time my partner anticipated the flight path of the ball and stuck her racquet out. My partner touched the return with her racquet which flew out of her hand. The ball ricocheted off the top of her racquet and took a piece of roof off of our gazebo in between courts #1 and #2. At this point, the returner had won eight points consecutively, however, the last point was the final point that she won. The following two points, the returner tried to lace the return down the line where she missed grossly wide and then long by ten plus feet. Even though she concluded her turn of ten points, I decided to keep pushing the envelope and had her stay returning serve. I ended up serving eleven more points of which she won none. All were lost on the return itself. My partner had destroyed the monstrosity of the forehand return by barely and unsuccessfully touching it. The returner's forehand was so connected to her ego that the mere fact someone would choose to cross its path unraveled her psyche/ forehand.

The epiphany was realized on the second return error the receiver blew long down the line and I bathed in the deconstruction of her forehand for the next eleven points. The revelation is as follows: If you can penetrate the physical façade of a ball striker and exploit the *caveman* ego fueling it, you can systematically destroy the weaponry. As long as there is no visual distraction, the ball striking returner will thrive. If the net player becomes enough of a visual distraction prior to the return, it will obstruct contact on the instinctive level.

The previous example that took place on my court speaks volumes in regards to players naturally becoming analytical and then finding comfort zones in response to what they are visually and physically experiencing. My net partner's instinct throughout the first seven points was to stay frozen in place allowing the returner to continually pound the return with a clear conscious. Because my net partner remained stagnant she imposed no visual distraction to the returner. More importantly she suggested no potential of movement, thus, her reach realm was never defined. On the eighth point, when my net partner decided to leave the cocoon she had spun for herself (her comfort zone), she rattled the returner's concentration and created a visual distraction for the returns to follow. Even though my net partner's attempt to poach was futile for that specific occasion, it implied that there was a potential for movement, therefore, establishing reach realm. It took time but my net partner turned her focus towards how she could possibly distract the returner. This decision was a premeditated act that diverted her attention outward, in the direction of her opponent, in contrast to the first seven points where she was consumed with the inward reaction set of self preservation. Within the structure of competitive tennis, it is necessary to inhibit the potential of a winning game plan from your opponents. Again, the communication line between the Logical Self and the Athletic Self, functions as a vital component to achieving this goal.

Chapter

12welve

S.A.F.E.T.Y.

---

this chapter's
approach

- Embracing distractions
- Defining S.A.F.E.T.Y.

The player or players, who win, in the game of tennis, are those competing with the clearest minds. The varieties of potential distractions that can divert attention and waiver concentration levels are infinite. In fact, I still encounter new sets of distractions through my student's accounts of their latest matches on a weekly basis. Traditionally, these distraction components have been labeled *excuses* where the term, in and of itself, carries a negative connotation. The problem with *excuses* is that they manifest into variables of gigantic proportions. They become objects or ideals that the psyche fixates upon to the point that competing becomes a secondary focus lost within the structure of a tennis match. It is important to recognize that some form of a distraction element will emerge in every match in which a player participates. Many of these potential *excuses* reoccur as constants that present themselves on a regular basis, however, there are others that players encounter that they have never been through.

Instead of distractions becoming synonymous with negativity, I propose tennis players should acknowledge, embrace, and then classify them categorically. If a competitor chooses to categorize their immediate distraction set, then they can properly focus on the most significant issue at hand: winning. I devised an acronym where each letter comprising the word **S.A.F.E.T.Y.** represents a significant and common arena of possible *excuses*. Collectively, S.A.F.E.T.Y. blankets every distraction dynamic a player could experience in the game of tennis. The following is the acronym and the words that compose it, housing all distraction components:

Sportsmanship

Act of God

Facility

Equipment

Tournament

Your preconceived perception of your opponents in relation to self

The category Sportsmanship is one of the most frequently referenced units of this acronym. Distraction factors within this domain include an opponent's physical and mental behavior, attitude, propensity to cheat, and even being too nice. Spectators including teammates, friends, family, or fans can also constitute Sportsmanship issues as they attempt to impose their will to influence the outcome of the tennis match. Another agent that should not be neglected due to its relevance is that of injury. A wilting psyche can manipulate an annoying ache into a critically acclaimed dramatic performance. Citing injury as an excuse to the influential factor of why a tennis match is won or lost, discredits play on the fundamental level.

The next classification set also causing distractions is Act of God. Within this category are variables that which a player and his opponent do not have any control. Typically, these elements include weather related issues such as strong winds, frigid temperatures, extreme heat, or rain which could delay play, inhibiting momentum runs for either side of the court. A competitor who is on the receiving end of an extremely lucky shot made by his opponent at an inopportune time may consider the event an Act of God. Roger Federer's between the legs passing shot from the baseline with his back facing his opponent, Novak Djokavic, in the 2009 U.S. Open Men's Semifinal to set up break point deep into the third set was amazing, entertaining, and clutch to the viewing audience. However, to Djokavic, this shot represented the proverbial "nail in the coffin" as he watched the missile of a passing shot scream by. When players perceive they are losing because forces beyond their control are waging war against them, their spirit tends to shatter. In Novak Djokavic's world that day, not only was Federer's performance sublime, as a whole, but he also possessed the capacity to play shots that caused even he to revel in wonder.

Excuses that embody the category, Facility, are virtually endless. Facility refers to issues players experience with surface type, maintenance concerns within the court structure, and the venue in general. Players who practice exclusively on hard courts have premeditated Facility anxieties about competing on clay courts or vice versa. A high percentage of Northerners and Midwesterners that vacation at Wild Dunes Resort in the fall through early spring always comment on the difficulties presented when moving from primarily indoor play to outdoor play. On occasion, a venue as a whole can carry a negative connotation as well. For example, if a player has lost the last three times he competed at a particular venue, that facility fosters a negative vibe to that particular player. This sentiment can subdue the competitive spirit as it conjures up previous experiences and weaves them into an emotional set.

The day before a match at Clemson University, our coach Chuck Kriese, always ended his speeches addressing the team with "Take care of the details!" This comment is representative of the fourth category in S.A.F.E.T.Y., which is Equipment. The tools we use to compete are in essence our armor and sword as we engage in battle. Racquets, strings, shoes, clothing, grips, and even vibration dampeners are all components embedded within this category. What Coach Kriese was referring to with his culminating comment of each speech was preparation on the finite level. It is important to never assume equipment is battle ready. A careful evaluation, from racquets to apparel, is necessary before any competitive match is played. When I was in the Boys 12 and under age division, I was playing in a State Championship event and I was in the semi-finals. My opponent, at the time, was someone I had never beaten before and I found myself leading the third set tiebreaker 4-2. At the beginning of the next point after I put my serve in play, the shoe lace on my right shoe broke. I was not carrying an additional pair of new shoe laces in my bag because it never dawned on me that my shoe laces would ever be an issue despite the fact that I dragged my right foot in an extreme fashion on all of my serves. I proceeded to lose the next five points in a row, falling to my demise by the score of 7-4 in the third set tiebreaker. From that point forward, I always carried a couple of spare sets of shoe laces in my bag. More importantly, I realized the significance of equipment and preparation and the impact it might have on the outcome of a tennis match. Instead of my focus being directed toward winning the match and competing, I became fixated on equipment failure which instigated defeat.

The category, Tournaments, is much more specific in nature with the distraction sets it may impose on a player. Most notably, a competitor has to be involved with a tournament to experience the potential mental diversions it may invoke. Unfavorable match times, tough draws, and bizarre T.A.E. (Tournament Administrative Errors) can all individually or collectively affect the way a player is able to compete. Also situated within the Tournament domain is the event itself. If a tournament represents tremendous importance to the player or if it is a higher level event than they are accustomed to playing, then it is common that nerves and self confidence interject a distraction element that cannot be reproduced on the practice court.

Probably the most abstract category of the six is Your Preconceived Perception of Your Opponents in Relation to Self. Pre-match anxiety will often pair with how the player perceives the level, reputation, or even attitudes of their opponent. In tennis tournaments, this distraction set runs rampant. Unseeded players who draw seeded players in the early rounds of an event announce their opponent as a seeded number rather than by name. The unseeded player might state, "I am playing the #1 seed," instead of "I am playing John Doe." Considering league matches, my students often refer to upcoming teams defined by their rating. A 3.0 woman comments, "We are playing a team composed of 3.5's that recently got bumped down." Both the tournament players and league players' remarks are factual, however, verbalizing their opponent's attributes prior to play does not allow for them to begin the match on an even playing field. The numeric label in front of a competitor's name or a league team can often construct mental hurdles that distract players from focusing on winning in a pure form. The reverse of this scenario is also true. An accomplished tennis player can fall prey to a dismissive attitude. They can easily underestimate their opponent's potential due to the perception they carry of their opponent's level or lack of experience. This line of thought can manifest into a subtle attitude of arrogance. When the tennis match begins and the first sign of adversity presents itself for the better player, he will begin to panic which can result in a massive distraction. Regardless of an opponent's ability level, all matches should be approached from the perspective of maintaining a proper and consistent line of respect. In doing so, potential perceptual distraction sets will be eliminated fostering an uninhibited competitive spirit.

Chapter
13teen

Momentum

I have always been fascinated by the concept of momentum. It is a force we cannot see, touch, taste, smell, or hear. The only empirical data that can be collected and recorded is score based information within a competitive sporting event. The emotional and corresponding physical attributes of being on the positive end of a momentum run include euphoria, rhythm, confidence, increased energy, and an imposing will. Collectively, these qualities nourish a winning spirit.

In my tennis clinics I always leave room towards the end for competitive match play analysis. I pair the students participating in the instruction into doubles teams and I have them play super tiebreakers. I like using super tiebreakers for match analysis purposes because there are very few played where a momentum run is not evident. Upon conclusion of the super tiebreaker I highlight strengths and weaknesses in strategy, court positioning, and stroke production. However, I emphasize where the super tiebreaker was won or lost. There is always a catalyst to a momentum run. I like to locate the initial spark that instigated the three...four...then five point run. I then make my students aware of three important factors that define momentum.

1. First and foremost, a tennis player has to acknowledge that momentum is very real

2. Second, there has to be an awareness of where you currently are with the score and how you got to that point

3. Third, you have to have the mental skill sets to combat the momentum moving against you and the ability to harness the momentum when it is on your side

It is embedded within this third factor where the leads are acquired and squandered, and tennis matches can swing in one direction or another. When a player or players are running with momentum on their side it is important to keep the tempo up in between points. When switching sides of the court it is necessary to set the pace quickly for their opponents to follow. Conversely, when momentum is against a player or doubles team and they experience their opponents taking control, the tempo must be slowed down in between points. The objective at this juncture is to upset and manipulate any rhythm their opponents may be enjoying.

The Logical Self and the Athletic Self have the inherent ability to both nurture and inhibit momentum. The equine world, once again, poses an interesting analogy to the Logical Self and the Athletic Self's ability to construct or deconstruct momentum. Imagine riding a cross country course on the back of an athletic presence such as a horse at top speed. As the equestrian approaches a 5' x 5' wooden fence natural fear instincts begin to present themselves. It is imperative to the success of the oncoming jump and the overall safety of both rider and animal that the proper information is passed from human to horse. In this case the Logical Self is the rider and the Athletic Self is the horse. Three strides out from the jump over the visually imposing wall the rider will sit back. Two strides out the rider will push his hands up and forward through the horse's mane. Finally, one stride out from the jump the rider will squeeze with both legs against the sides of the horse to physically stimulate an acceleration command. Each physical gesture timed appropriately to the stride in proximity of the jump is specific and direct. There is a learned trust factor between the human and horse that produces a rhythm, harmony, and confident approach to this potentially dangerous athletic event.

Using the same equestrian example, but imposing a different communication set or vibe between the rider and the horse, a completely different response could result. If the rider or horse is "green," a trust factor has not been established. As the pair moves toward an upcoming jump and the rider gives way to natural fear instincts, the horse will sense tension and panic from the rider on a physiological level. The rider's panic can also produce inaccurate physical gestures that could be interpreted by the horse as a command in conjunction with spontaneous and inappropriate audible cues that can further complicate the oncoming jump. Typically, this kind of reaction issued from the rider disrupts the athletic event causing the horse to stop abruptly or even take off in a different direction.

The horse is clearly a physical extension of its rider. This athletic machine responds to a set of physical and audible commands within the realm of trust. When trust is disabled through over analysis and panic, so is the symmetry between horse and rider, or the Athletic Self and the Logical Self.

The previous two analogies mirror the relationship between the Logical Self and the Athletic Self during competition and more specifically what is mentally and physically experienced through either side of a momentum run in tennis. Players on the positive side of a momentum run realize rhythm, harmony, and confident approach to their competitive endeavor. The proverbial "zone" is entered where the Logical Self may loosely manage the Athletic Self. The tennis player attains a sense of trust where feel and rhythm permeate the competitive arena. In contrast, the competitor on the negative end of a momentum run will encounter panic driven action through over analysis. The Logical Self and the Athletic Self are at odds due to one thinking at the speed of light and the other attempting to act upon it. This reactive analysis derived from the Logical Self disables the trust factor and dismantles the performance potential of the Athletic Self.

The skill sets involved to combat negative momentum which has turned against you are predominantly mental. A player or doubles team must disengage the natural tendency to over analyze and properly redirect their focus to their current physical position on the tennis court. Remember each position, in doubles especially, bears a set of responsibilities that include court positioning, shot selection, and movement patterns. In conjunction with slowing the tempo down in an effort to disrupt any rhythm the opponents may be experiencing, it is imperative that the players also acknowledge their responsibility sets by working through a mental progression. Our analysis distracts the tennis player from focus and execution. Action commands and a mental progression equip the Logical Self with the tools to direct the Athletic Self in a centered and productive fashion.

Harnessing momentum is vague. The challenge is for the Logical Self to loosely manage the Athletic Self which enables trust and confidence. Any form of analysis has the potential of derailing a momentum run. There is a rhythm that tennis players experience when they are in control of a tennis match and thereby, running with momentum. This rhythm is only acknowledged if the mind is clear from **chatter**. I have recently started alluding to the thoughts that run through a tennis players mind as chatter. The chatter in a competitor's head is what can ultimately lead to the demise of a tennis match. It is one of the most intense forms of distraction that exist for any player. Chatter rarely has any positive overtones, thus, it is mostly critical and negative. The easiest way to eliminate chatter is through positive energy. Positive energy is born through movement, specifically abundant and robust footwork. If a competitor is moving at a high level, relatively speaking, then all of their focus is directed toward that aspect of the game. Chatter is quelled and rhythm flows.

Chapter

14teen

Practice

The great Hall of Fame football coach of the Green Bay Packers, Vince Lombardi, once quipped, "Practice does not make perfect. Perfect practice makes perfect." The practice court is where the foundation is built for every tennis player. I believe that there should be very specific and routine driven preparation for practice. The same anxieties, pressures, and emotions that are evident before match play must be projected onto the practice court. In doing so, when the day of a match presents itself the competitor has truly been there before qualifying, the practice court as important, if not more important, than the match court. The ability to project match-like paradigms to the practice realm is a learned trait. Competitors have to experience match play, collect stressor and distraction agents, and then impose them through the practice court. Too often I see players on the practice court going through the motions on auto pilot. Although on the cardiovascular level it presents a quality workout, it is in no way representative of what transpires mentally or emotionally during match play. Competitors must be accountable during practice, and only then is match play simulated and of true value.

The practice court should also include the dialogue between the Logical Self and the Athletic Self. Action commands and mental progressions need to become natural reference points and continually re-visited throughout the extent of a practice session. Repetition with this level of focus is a fundamental cornerstone to growth. I often allude to the development of tennis players as comparable to "watching paint dry on a wall." The process is extremely slow, methodical, and specific. In private lessons, I may work on maturing one, and no more than two, action commands at a time. If the student, on his own, is deliberate with his practice sessions, in an attempt to reinforce a skill set, months could go by before an athletic process becomes natural. In fact, some mental progressions such as serving and moving forward, become only moderately functional at best for some people regardless of how much time they allocate towards perfection. Whether discussing action commands or mental progressions as growth factors, maximizing an individual's potential is realized through years and years of successes found in the smallest increments. Thousands of baby steps could eventually translate into miles; however, the process to a theorctical destination must be appreciated and enjoyed.

I have been entrenched in the sport of tennis since I was two years old. I often joke to others that I do not know anything else. However, I have learned that tennis is a reflection of life. Typically, nothing comes easily and when successes are achieved we recognize the hard work and the long road that went into realizing that success. Losses represent growth opportunities. They pinpoint weaknesses and motivate the core competitor inside each of us to better ourselves through training and experience. As tennis relates to life, I find myself constantly evolving as a person, tennis player, and instructor / coach. Recognizing the mental components woven throughout these chapters will hopefully provide tools that will lead toward a path of maximizing one's potential.

Action Commands

Terms the Logical Self uses to communicate to the Athletic
Self to perform a specific action during an athletic event.
The term is typically simple in nature but carries sub layers of
information that the Logical Self packages into the spirit of a command.

The Athletic Self

It's the reactive, undisciplined state of panic each time the ball is put in play
in a competitive fashion. Once competing begins, the Athletic Self takes
over, hence, our more primitive state of mind rules all decision making.

Auto Pilot

The term "auto pilot" refers to the Athletic Self taking over any physical
endeavor, whether in the practice or the competitive modes.

Brain Alignment

Operates on the theory that in a competitive arena, such as tennis, we are
two selves: The Logical Self and The Athletic Self.

Chatter

The thoughts that run through a tennis players mind. Typically, chatter
has negative overtones and is one of the most intense forms of distraction
for any player.

Comfort Zones

A "comfort zone" is the Athletic Self's instinctive and emotive based
physical response to any set of internal or external stimuli.

Dynamic Court Positioning

The movement pattern performed off of a recovery shot into the proper new court positioning trend based on the rules of Staggered Formation.

First Exchange

Traditionally the first two shots exchanged or struck in any given point.

The I Woulda Coulda Shoulda Moments

The disappointment experienced upon reflection of a shot that traveled through a players perceived reach realm that they did not move on.

If...then Statements

The mental progression practiced by the more reactive positions of the court. Generating insight based on the serving team's trends establishes a game plan that creates proactive guidelines in a reactive setting.

Inside Wing

The inside wing is the side where the ball striking is closest to the center of the court (the left side from the deuce court perspective and the right side from the ad court perspective) whether the opponent is left or right handed. The inside wing breeds little shot selection from your opponents.

The Logical Self

It is the rational, thoughtful, potentially proactive, and understanding Self that has time to digest, process, and regurgitate information. The Logical Self rules the court in most occasions until the ball is put in play.

Mental Progression

A dialogue between the Logical Self and the Athletic Self before each point is played that functions as court positioning awareness and the subset of responsibilities that it entails. Engaging in a mental progression prior to a point being played is the foundation of proactive tennis.

Outside the Box

Instead of the receiver lining up with in the geometric lines of the tennis court, it's important they face their core in line with the server. The natural swing plane does not change, but by creating this angle, the returner is able to manipulate the direction of the return away from the server's partner.

Outside Wing

The side furthest from the center of the court (the right side from the deuce court perspective and the left side from the ad court perspective) and the side that creates the greatest amount of shot selection.

Reach Realm

The perceived distance the server's partner will move to intercept a return of serve.

Reactive Analysis

Thinking with the Logical Self while the athletic event is in motion. This thinking crosses the wires of Logical Self and Athletic Self typically debilitating the potentially natural and fluid actions.

Recall Buttons

The foundation of experience. In its fundamental sense, it is the ability to download an experience or a set of circumstances into our memory bank which can be accessed, with a label, by the Logical Self.

Recovery Shot

A shot exercised when a player is out of position and needs to buy time to recover proper court positioning.

S.A.F.E.T.Y.

An acronym where each letter represents a significant and common arena of possible excuses. Collectively, this acronym blankets every distraction dynamic a player could experience in the game of tennis.

The Server and Receiver's Triangle

Look at the vertical net strap, located in the center of the net, and look through the net to see where it intersects with the horizontal service line. Then observe the vertical service line (bisecting the two service boxes) from the "T" and visually bring it back to the net strap, there is a triangle that we can use as a hitting point target. This triangle exists on both the deuce and the ad side and the further you move from the center hash mark on the baseline the larger the triangle gets.

Shot Tolerance

Represents the receiver's ability to stay steadfast to one target with their shot selection until an outcome or opportunity is realized.

Sleep Walk

The Athletic Self's attempt to migrate into an area of the court where it perceives it has the most time to react.

Staggered Formation

Staggered Formation is a system of doubles court positioning that arms both partners with a knowledge base equipped with shot selection and movement patterns. It is a proactive style of play that turns the focus inward where execution is the dominating factor.

Static Court Positioning

The lack of movement or sleep walking into a comfort zone after a recovery shot has been played.

The Three F's

Three categories (Feet, Focus, and Feel) that comparmentalize virtually all action commands.

34737331R00065

Made in the USA
Middletown, DE
02 September 2016